contents

Above: **Jam Master Jay and his son. Manhattan, 1988.**

Right: **Roxanne Shante, Manhattan, 1987 (left), and LL Cool J, Manhattan, 1985.**

Top left: **EPMD, Manhattan, 1988.** *Second from top, left:* **Heavy D & the Boyz, Manhattan, 1990.** *Below:* **Public Enemy, Manhattan, 1988.**

Below: **KRS-One and Ms. Melodie, husband and wife. The Bronx, 1989.**

rap!

UTFO's Dr. Ice. Brooklyn, 1986.

D1

Native Tongues Posse. Manhattan, 1990.

rap!

**portraits and
lyrics of a
generation of
black rockers**

photographs by
janette beckman
text by b. adler
foreword by doctor
dre and ed lover of
"yo! mtv raps"

st. martin's press / new york

RAP: PORTRAITS AND LYRICS OF A GENERATION OF BLACK ROCKERS. Copyright © 1991 by B. Adler and Janette Beckman. All rights reserved. Printed in the United States of America. No part of this book may be used or reproduced in any manner whatsoever without written permission except in the case of brief quotations embodied in critical articles or reviews. For information, address St. Martin's Press, 175 Fifth Avenue, New York, N.Y. 10010.

Design by Jaye Zimet

Library of Congress Cataloging-in-Publication Data

Beckman, Janette.
    Rap : portraits and lyrics of a generation of black rockers /
photographs by Janette Beckman : text by B. Adler : foreword by
Doctor Dre and Ed Lover.
        p. cm.
    ISBN 0-312-05501-3 (pbk.)
    1. Rap (Music)—Pictorial works.   2. Rap musicians—Portraits.
    3. Rap (Music)—Texts.   I. Adler, B.   II. Title.
    ML3531.B4 1991
    782.42164—dc20
                                                                              90-49960
                                                                                   CIP

First Edition: March 1991
10 9 8 7 6 5 4 3 2 1

To my parents, Pauline and Michael Beckman, who bought me my first Tamla/ Motown records.

—Janette Beckman

To my children, Ruth and Sam Adler, delighted young citizens of the Black Planet.

—B. Adler

Cash Money & MC Marvelous. Philadelphia, 1987.

Tone Loc, Los Angeles, 1990.

X   **Rock Steady Crew, breakdancers. Harlem, 1983.**

acknowledgments

Antoinette. Manhattan, 1988.

Given that Janette Beckman has been photographing rappers since 1982, much of the hard work involved with a project like this was completed well before the book itself was a gleam in anyone's eye. Even so, there were a number of important artists whom Janette had not shot by January of 1990, when *Rap* got off the ground, and it is to these acts that we extend our first vote of thanks: Queen Latifah, MC Lyte, the 2 Live Crew, Ice-T, Ice Cube, NWA, Tone Loc, Young MC, the Boo-Yaa Tribe, Dr. Jeckyll & Mr. Hyde, and Heavy D & the Boyz.

Fervent thanks, of course, to our agent, Lori Perkins, and to our editor, Jim Fitzgerald at St. Martin's Press.

We had a ton of help from our friends and colleagues in the music industry, including: Carmen Ashhurst-Watson, Def Jam Recordings; Heidi Smith, Rush Artist Management; Debbie Bennett, Luke's Records; Lillian Matulic, Priority Records; Madeleine Smith, Ruthless Attack Muzick; Tracey Miller and Gary Pini, Profile Records; Dave "Funken" Klein and Red Alert, Red Alert Productions; Eddie O'Loughlin, Jenniene Leclercq, Judy Herman, Jenny Buermann, Next Plateau Records; Eloise Bryan, Shelby Meade, and Vivian Robinson, MCA Records; Rene Foster, Uptown Enterprises; Cindy Gray and Denise Cox, Island Records; J. B. Moore; Monica Lynch and Laura Hynes, Tommy Boy Records; Duane Taylor and Sean Carasov, Jive Records; Will Socolov and Valerie Harper, Sleeping Bag Records; Fred Munao and Ursula Smith, Select Records; Terry Moorer, First Priority Records; Monica Mechium, Cold Chillin' Records; Tony Johnson, LaTanya White, Warner Brothers Records; Angela Thomas, Mary Ellen Cataneo, Jim Merlis, Judy Watson, Columbia Records; Simo Doe, Atlantic Records; Jorge Hinojosa and Donald D of Rhyme Syndicate; Bill Stephney, Lindsey Williams, Walter Dawkins, SOUL: Sound of Urban Listeners; Patrick Moxey, Wild Pitch Records; the Flavor Unit; Toni Green of Pretty Special Inc., Leyla Turkkan and Grace Heck, STR Public Relations; and Zoe Brotman and April Garston of Icon Design.

Thanks to Joseph "Run" Simmons of Run-DMC, Mike D of the Beastie Boys, Parrish Smith of EPMD, MC Lyte, Posduuos of De La Soul, Rakim of Eric B. & Rakim, and DST for help with the transcription of their lyrics.

Thanks to music writers Dan Charnas of *The Source* (for his transcription of "The Nigga Ya Love to Hate"), John Leland of *New York Newsday,* Joe Levy of the *Village Voice,* Peter Carlson of the *Washington Post Magazine,* Vivien Goldman and Paolo Hewitt of England's *New Musical Express,* and Frank Owen of *Spin.*

We'd also like to acknowledge the following writers, from whose interviews with notable rappers we fished for quotes: Greg Sandow, *Village Voice* (interviews with Ice-T, NWA, Tone Loc); Bob Hilburn, *Los Angeles Times* (Ice Cube); Jonathan Gold, *L.A. Weekly* (NWA); Patrick Goldstein, *Los Angeles Times* (Boo-Yaa Tribe); David Toop, *The Face* (Boo-Yaa Tribe); Marie Elsie St. Leger, *Ear* (Queen Latifah); Wendy Blatt, *DJ Times* (Rob Base); Steve Blush, *Seconds* (KRS-One). Steven Hager's invaluable *Hip Hop: The Illustrated History of Breakdancing, Rap Music, and Graffiti* (St. Martin's Press, 1984) was the source of all of the quotes used for the chapter on Kool Herc.

Special thanks to the "Yo! MTV Raps" posse for all of their support and advice: Doctor Dre (and Solomon Petersen) and Ed Lover, Fab 5 Freddy, Ted Demme, and Moses Edinborough.

Very special thanks to Nicole Payen, the one-woman staff of Rhyme & Reason Communications, for her dedication, zeal, humor, and attention to a thousand and one crucial details...and to Ambassador Bonz Malone, the Knight of Stone, for his transcription of a number of the lyrics reprinted here.

Bill's extra special thanks radiate, as ever, to Sara Moulton, his wife, his soul mate, his angel. Janette's extra special thanks go out to photo editor Ginger Canzoneri for her taste, positivity, inspiration, and encouragement throughout this project.

Special thanks to Lyor Cohen of Rush Artists Management for coming through in a pinch and helping us to secure the cooperation of our cover subject, Big Daddy Kane, to whom we will always be eternally grateful.

Doctor Dre and Ed Lover. Manhattan, 1989.

foreword

by doctor dre and ed lover of "yo! mtv raps"

We've both been involved with hip-hop since way before there were rap records, and if anybody had ever told us then that the music would turn into *all this* or that we'd be on television hosting a whole show about rap . . . well, we woulda known he was out of his mind. [Confession from Doctor Dre: "Bullshit! I always knew it was gonna blow up!"] The amazing thing is that we're having as much fun with it now—when rap is *everywhere we go*—as we did in junior high, when rap was just this little underground thing. It sures beats working.

Janette's photos are *def,* but we've known that for a while. Dre met Janette when he needed some publicity shots for Original Concept, and the two of us and T-Money all got with her when we needed some fly new flicks of us for "Yo." There's never been a book like this on rap before, a book with rhymes and photos and bios, a book that treats the artists with respect, but now there is . . .

. . . REAL DEF!!

C-Ya!
Doctor Dre and Ed Lover

Doctor Dre, Ed Lover, and T-Money. Manhattan, 1989.

Hurby Luv Bug and the Idolmakers posse: Salt 'n' Pepa, Kid 'n' Play, Dana Dane, Sweet T, Antoinette, Non Stop, Steevee-O, Hurby Luv Bug, Clark Kent, Ron Won, Prince Sundance, and Candy. Manhattan, 1989.

introduction

Top: **Joe-Ski Love (obviously). Manhattan 1990.** *Bottom:* **World Famous Supreme Team. At the Roxy, Manhattan, 1984.**

In the spring of 1990 a pay-TV concert special entitled "Rapmania" celebrated the fifteenth anniversary of the birth of rap. Fifteen years is a long time in popular culture, time enough for several generations, indeed for entire revolutions, to flower and fade. Think of rock 'n' roll at fifteen, circa 1971: the music was posivitely middle-aged. Jimi Hendrix dead, Jim Morrison dead, Janis Joplin dead, the Beatles broken up . . . with Carole King, James Taylor, and Crosby, Stills & Nash left to battle it out at the top of the charts, and Elton John looming on the horizon. Gruesome.

Rap, by contrast, may be more fiery now, and more creative, than at any time in its past. Surely the passions it inspires, both pro and con, have never run deeper. It is adored by millions in the streets and reviled by hundreds in the suites. It is boycotted by both "rock" and "black" radio and endorsed by MTV (whose "Yo! MTV Raps" is the music channel's most highly rated show) and NBC television (which is building a prime-time show around the charisma of the Fresh Prince). It has been saluted by Jesse Jackson and denounced by the Parents Music Resource Center and Focus on the Family. It has been embraced by the National Urban League (the beneficiaries of the proceeds from the Stop the Violence Movement's "Self-Destruction" record and video) and condemned by the PTA. It was hailed by the *Village Voice* in February 1990 after their annual national poll of 250 music critics resulted in a rap album at the top of the heap, and assailed by *Newsweek* magazine the following month in a hatchet job of a cover story entitled "Rap Rage." Cultural conservatives swear it's illiterate, but Dr. Houston Baker of the University of Pennsylvania suggests that the real illiterates are those college professors who don't follow it and who yet somehow hope to connect with their students. The FBI goes after NWA because the Bureau is convinced that the rappers' song "[Fuck] tha Police" encourages violence against police officers, but millions of black kids all across the country applaud it as a kind of audio documentary of everyday police brutality in their communities. Most recently, a federal judge in Florida declared the 2 Live Crew's "As Nasty as They Wanna Be" obscene, and a local record store owner who disagreed defiantly continued to sell it and then cheerfully went to jail in support of it. In short, fifteen years after its birth, rap—just like the greatest rock 'n' roll before it—continues to pose the question: Which side are you on?

This is a book by and for people who love rap. And if it does nothing else, it'll convince people who only know what they read in the newspapers (or what they watch on television) that there's more—much more—than one dimension to rap. A simple flip through the pages should be enough to demonstrate that there's at least as much visual variety and development in rap music as there's ever been in any other subgenre of rock . . . and considerably more than there was in, say, folk music or glitter rock. We are, after all, talking about fifteen years' worth of history and hundreds of notable artists.

The truth is that most of us who love this music don't even think of it in terms of genre. Nobody goes into a record store thinking, "I've got twenty-five dollars. I'm gonna buy two tapes by rappers and two by singers." We think in terms of *individual artists:* "Who's hot right now?"

Top: **Schooly D. Manhattan, 1986.** *Bottom:* **King Sun and D. Moet. Harlem, 1987.**

Still, to the extent that we do think collectively about these artists, consider how much diversity and uniqueness is captured in these pages: the sweetness of Salt 'n' Pepa and the bitterness of Ice Cube, the homeboy camaraderie of Run-DMC and the competitiveness of LL Cool J, the gangster menace of Eric B & Rakim and the visionary openness of the Jungle Brothers, the blazing anger of Public Enemy and the playfulness of Kid 'n' Play, the frat-boy sexism of the 2 Live Crew and the feminist pride of Queen Latifah, the cartoon goofiness of the Fat Boys and the simple dignity of Heavy D, the self-conscious ebony beauty of Big Daddy Kane and the proud nerdiness of De La Soul, the everyday casual cool of EPMD and the exotic tribalism of the Boo-Yaas, the slightly starchy righteousness of KRS-ONE and the let-it-all-hang-out humor of Tone Loc, etc., etc., etc.

As a written and visual complement of actual rap records and concerts, this book demonstrates that rap—the great rock 'n' roll of its day—is rich with all of the qualities that have always made rock 'n' roll great: big beats, sex, wit, humor, nonsense, adolescent rebelliousness, grown-up revolutionary slo-ganeering, wild haircuts, cool clothes, and more sex. And, like all of the greatest rock 'n' roll, it opens up the possibility of escape: escape from dreary middle-class convention and deadly underclass desperation alike.

Indeed, even the most apolitical rap has been a tonic, especially to black youth. It was, after all, conceived as a pure expression of the black youth of New York City, a protest against the terrifying popular music of the mid-to-late 1970s: disco. The ridiculously rich vein of soul and funk mined throughout the Sixties and into the early Seventies was nearly tapped out, and in its place came Donna Summer, the Bee Gees and their brother Andy Gibb, Abba, Rick Dees and His Cast of Idiots, Leo Sayer, Alicia Bridges, the Village People, Gloria Gaynor, Thelma Houston, Amii Stewart, ad nauseam. To be fair, these artists were virtually interchangeable; the Seventies was the Era of the Producer. But even bigger than any given producer was that deadly, maniacal disco beat. A nightmare! Thousands of records, hundreds of hits, and every single one of them driven by the same jackhammer of industrial rhythm! A beat that pounded away, four beats per measure, 120 beats per minute—*pound pound pound pound pound pound pound*—as predictable as death and taxes and nearly as hard to swallow. A beat purportedly designed for dancers that generated the spirit of free-flowing body improvisation about as readily as the U.S. Marine Corps Marching Band! A beat to split one's head open! A beat for robots and stiffs!

But though the rest of the world may have marched to it—what else *was* there?—the black teens of the Bronx weren't going for it. The Bronx, or at least the South Bronx, was a virtual model of urban decay. When Ronald Reagan whistlestopped it during his presidential campaign in 1980, the pol with a head of wood and a heart of stone was moved to declare that he hadn't seen devastation on a scale like that "since London after the Blitz" (an observation which probably said more about Reagan's isolation and ignorance than about the singularity of the Bronx). But whatever the natives may have lacked in the basic necessities of life, they certainly didn't lack taste. In a world given over

Dana Dane. Manhattan, 1987.

to the rhythmic fascism of the Machine, funk was where you found it. And so it was up to the first great geniuses of rap—party deejays like Kool Herc, Afrika Bambaataa, Grand Master Flash, Grand Wizard Theodore, Pete "DJ" Jones, and DJ Hollywood—to pick through the auto graveyard of the previous twenty years' worth of pop in a dedicated search for enough cool parts to build a serviceable new ride. Rock, jazz, soul, TV themes and advertising jingles, drumbeats, bass lines, piano parts, horn charts, guitar riffs...and every kind of frenzied human voice looking to drive dancers nuts by shouting some variation on *"Uh, get up, uh get-get get down!"* (as Flavor Flav does on Public Enemy's "911 Is a Joke")—they all went into the mix. The trick was to reassemble those parts in such a way as to generate what the great Bootsy Collins once described as *high butt pleasure.* And even then, all you had was the beat—and a beat without a rhyme is not rap.

Rap music eats up lyrics at a rate of about four times what the usual pop song requires—which suits most rappers just fine. A perusal of the lyrics on the following pages demonstrates a sheer love of language unlike anything else you'll find in contemporary pop. It is a jailbreak, it is a dam bursting, it is beautfiul and it is profane, it is poetry and it is journalism. And it is also deeply unsettling to the powers that be. For the first time in twenty years, rap is allowing young black voices to be heard. The FBI, in the form of the Cointelpro program, systematically shut down the sounds of protest from the black community at the end of the Sixties. Now all of a sudden, after a generation of formula pap, the air is rent by a torrent of unauthorized transmissions: *"Don't push me 'cause I'm close to the edge," "I'm bad," "I'm black and I'm proud and I'm full of ambition," "Me so horny," "Fuck the police," "Parents just don't understand," "911 is a joke," "We didn't kill 'im, we painted him black," "You must learn," "Burn, Hollywood, burn!" "A woman can bear you, break you, take you," "Wild thing!" "How can I move the crowd," "South Africa no free, neither are we," "You gots to chill," "The cops shot the kid, I can still hear him scream," "Stop the violence," "Fight the power!" "Doowutchyalike."*

Even resolutely apolitical rappers like LL Cool J pose a threat. Unlike the R & B stars who preceded him, LL doesn't wear a spangled tuxedo, doesn't smile when you point a camera at him, doesn't even *sing*—and yet there he is selling millions of records, grinding away on television, grinning down at someone's daughter from a poster on the wall of her bedroom. For ten years Bill Cosby and the Cosby kids have defined black life for white America. Rap bumrushed the show and all of a sudden it was clear that there were *many* ways to be black in America, most of which appeared to be considerably more amusing and considerably deeper (or, at the least, considerably more real) than the one authorized by oppressive old Ghost Dad Bill and his friends in the Positive Image Mentality Police.

The Positive Image Mentality is what makes rap just as threatening to older middle-class blacks as it is to older middle-class whites. Nelson George, the writer who identified the syndrome, notes: "PIM is tunnel vision that sees all success stories as benefiting the race—role models for the young, proof we can compete on white terms. It is an elitist worldview that serves establishment blacks . . . but doesn't help the black masses." The kind of musicians held up by PIM include Luther Vandross, Anita Baker, and Whitney Houston, artists who are well groomed, smiley, and devoted to love songs, nothing but love songs. PIM hates rap because it's nappy, pissed-off, loud, lewd, irreverent, confrontational, and inclined to address every ugly and beautiful subject under the sun, moon, and stars. Public Enemy's Chuck D is devoted to rap because he understands it as "black America's CNN," because it is the one medium that can be counted on to get the news out to kids all over the country about how other kids in other communities are living, because, in short, it makes Ralph Ellison's Invisible Man visible (and audible) again for the first time in a generation.

Then again, rap is rock, after all, and rock has *always* been at least incidentally about pissing off the old folks. Hank Ballard and the Midnighters, the 2 Live Crew of their day, saw their record "Annie Had a Baby" declared obscene and banned. Elvis Presley's performance on "The Ed Sullivan Show" was censored from the waist down. The Beatles claimed that they were more popular than Jesus and America's Bible Belt fundamentalists made bonfires of their records. The authorities tend to fuck with rock 'n' roll because they understand that the music is essentially antiauthoritarian. These days black *and* white kids sport the T-shirt that sums up the current situation: "It's a black thing; you wouldn't understand."

That's why we all owe a debt of gratitude to "Yo! MTV Raps." For all of the music's barrier-busting achievements prior to January 1989, rap was virtually born anew with the debut of "Yo!" For the first time, after ten years of great records that remained little more than a rumor to the masses of white record-buying kids, rap was real. More than that, rap's superiority to the bulk of the "rock" portioned out to white kids was obvious. Young rockers were finally getting a chance to do some comparison shopping. Sandwiched every day after school between "Club MTV" and "The Hard 30," "Yo!" kicked much ass: more danceable than the "dance music" showcased on "Club" and harder than the "hard rock" that followed it. Suddenly, it was unmistakable: whatever it is about rock that compelled the love and loyalty of generations of kids, rap had it (yes!) in spades.

Of course, all of this is predicated on an Afrocentric understanding of the history of rock. If, like the whitebreads who program AOR radio, you believe that rock proceeds from Elvis to the Beatles and the Who to Led Zeppelin and Elton John and finally to Bon Jovi and Phil Collins, then rap is not only not going to fit your definition of rock, it likely won't even qualify as music. On the other hand, if your hall of fame runs from Little Richard and Bo Diddley to James Brown and Jimi Hendrix and Sly & the Family Stone, to Kool and the Gang and Parliament/Funkadelic and finally to Prince and the heroes of hip-hop, then you're going to understand that rap is strictly *in the tradition.*

The larger problem is that American society today is nearly as segregated as it was at the beginning of the rock era in the mid-Fifties. Today's white youth comprise the first generation since World War II to have come of age without any significant exposure to African-American music as played by African Amer-

Red Alert, left, with two-thirds of the Jungle Brothers. Manhattan, 1990.

Stetsasonic. Brooklyn, 1988.

icans. But just as rock 'n' roll sparked the integration of America ten years before the establishment of the Civil Rights acts of 1964 and 1965, rap, via "Yo! MTV Raps," is beginning to bring the races together in the Nineties. Tone Loc, Rob Base, and Salt 'n' Pepa were no less alien to white kids in Idaho at the end of the Eighties than Little Richard—the original brother from another planet—had been to their parents in 1956. But Little Richard *slayed* the white competition of his day. Likewise, rap waxes its competition today. As ever, it is impossible to miss the excitement of the real thing, and young white kids have taken to rap in direct proportion to their exposure to it.

And, by the way, there's no discounting the contributions of the "Yo!" veejays: Doctor Dre and Ed Lover on weekdays, Fab 5 Freddy on Saturdays. Just as Alan Freed won his place in history by being the first rock 'n' roll deejay to insist on playing nothing for his young white and black audience but the records of the music's black originators, so too Ed and Dre and Fred. Kids *love* these guys, especially given the competition. How is Adam Curry or Martha Quinn supposed to compete with the Cheech and Chong earthiness, the humor and hipness of Dre and Ed . . . or with the avant-garde styling and cool of Fab 5 Freddie? And let's not forget Ted Demme and Peter Dougherty, the young men of the Caucasian persuasion who first sold "Yo!" to MTV. They are indeed mighty whiteys.

Enjoy the book. It is arranged more or less chronologically to provide a kind of condensed history of the music. We were as comprehensive as possible given the usual logistical and financial limitations, but there are lots of artists we would have included if we only could have. (And lots more rhymes, as well.) Certainly, our major omissions include: the Cold Crush Brothers, Spoonie Gee, the Treacherous Three and Kool Moe Dee, the Funky Four Plus One, Busy Bee, Whodini, Kwame, the Audio Two, Jazzy Jeff & the Fresh Prince, Biz Markie, the Cookie Crew, Gang Starr, the Afros, Digital Underground, Sir Mix-A-Lot, Kid Frost, Mellow Man Ace, Poor Righteous Teachers, the Young Black Teenagers, and MC Hammer. But, what the hell, maybe we'll get a shot at Volume Two some day. Assuming we can stall off the second coming of Cointelpro, rap figures to be around for quite a while yet.

B. Adler
New York City
July 1, 1990

Left: **Two-thirds of the Sugar Hill Gang: Wonder Mike, center, and Master Gee, left. Tryone Black-man is at right. Big Bank Hank was missing-in-action.**

"Rapmania"—1990

"Rapmania" was conceived as an extravagant fifteenth birthday party for the music. Produced by Van Silk (a Bronx-born promoter, manager, and rapper who was present at the creation) in honor of founding father Kool Herc, the show assembled forty of the most notable acts in rap's history for simultaneous concerts in New York at the Apollo Theatre and in Los Angeles at the Hollywood Palace on March 9, 1990. Old-schoolers like Melle Mel, Kurtis Blow, Afrika Bambaataa, and the Sugar Hill Gang performed on the same bill with new kids like Young MC and Kwame. Superstars like LL Cool J performed on the same bill with relative unknowns like Twin Hype. The idea, according to Van Silk, was not only to celebrate the longevity and health of the music, but to demonstrate that "the rap world could come together without animosity, just as the movie and television worlds do." Indeed, such ancient antagonists as LL Cool J/Kool Moe Dee and Roxanne Shante/the Real Roxanne buried the hatchet at "Rapmania."

Janette set up a makeshift little photo booth backstage in the press room at the Apollo and snapped away at all of the artists who wandered in. The show was aired on pay-TV on April 6.

L'il Bam

2 **Red Alert**

Wanda D & Company

Special Ed

A Little Jamm

5

6

Jazzy Joyce

The Kwame Dancers

Double Vision

The Wise Guys

10

Digger Dan

12

The Zulu Nation Dancers

rap!

Lovebug Starski. Manhattan, 1986.

14

At "Rapmania," 1990.

kool herc

Kool Herc was born Clive Campbell in Kingston, Jamaica, and moved with his family to the Bronx as a twelve-year-old in 1967. In 1975 he started giving parties at a teen nightclub called the Hevalo, at 180th Street and Jerome Avenue in the Bronx. He is widely acknowledged as the first rap deejay.

"I went to the Hevalo when I was thirteen," remembers the Sisco Kid. "Everybody was lined up around the block. They had a gangster look and were older than me. I said, 'Oh, shit! This is crazy!' It was very dark inside, but there was an excitement in the air, like anything could jump off. You'd see some dude dancing and he'd be wearing alligator shoes. Then Herc came on the mike and he was so tough. You'd get transfixed by his shit. You thought, 'This is cool. I want to be like this.' "

"Kevin" says: "The thing I mostly remember was how loud the music was. The sound overtook you. The place was packed—a real sweatbox. Herc would call out the names of people at the party: Wallace Dee, Johnny Cool, Chubby, the Amazing Bobo, James Bond, Sasa, Clark Kent, Trixie. Trixie had a big afro and he used to shake his head. It used to make him look so *good!* Wallace Dee had a move called the Slingshot, which was a basic drop to the floor, except he came up like he was shooting a slingshot. There was no such thing as b-boys when we arrived, but Herc gave us that tag, just like he named his sound system the Herculords and he called me and my brother the Nigger Twins."

Grandmaster Flash remembers: "I would go to the Hevalo sometimes to check Herc out, but Herc used to embarrass me quite a bit. He'd say, 'Grandmaster Flash in the house' over the mike, and then he'd cut off the highs and lows on his system and just play the midrange.

" 'Flash,' he'd say. 'In order to be a qualified disc jockey, there is one thing you must have . . . *highs!*' Then Herc would crank up his highs and the high hat would be sizzling. 'And most of all, Flash,' he'd say, 'you must have . . . *bass!*' Well, when Herc's bass came in the whole place would be shaking. I'd get so embarrassed that I'd have to leave. My system couldn't compare."

By 1977, with Flash and his Furious Three emcees in the ascendancy, Herc was becoming less popular. Then Herc got stabbed at one of his own parties. "The party hadn't even started," he recalls. "Three guys came to the door and my people wouldn't let them in. They said they was looking for the owner. A discrepancy started. By this time I'm finished dressing and I walk over and say, 'What's happening?' *Boom, boom, boom!* I got stabbed three times, once in the hand and twice in the side. The guy with the knife was drunk. Somebody stabbed him up, but I'm sorry to say he lived. I took a piece of ice, put it on my side, and walked to the hospital.

"After that the door was open for Flash. How do you think people feel about coming to a party when the host gets stabbed? Then my place burned down. Papa couldn't find no good ranch, so his herd scattered."

15

16

Top: **Fab 5 Freddy and the Rammellzee. London, 1982.** *Bottom:* **Grandmixer DST and the Infinity Rappers. Left to right: Shaheem, DST, and the Godfather KC. London, 1982.**

"the new york city rap tour" in europe, 1982

From "Change the Beat" by Fab 5 Freddy

The hip-hop world is a fantasy
Groovin' to the rhythms of reality
Just a grabbin' the mike and takin' control
Being the monumental master, playin' the
role
Pullin' the curtains back and lettin' you
know
That when I'm on the mike, I'm rockin' the
show

**From "Mega Mix 2 (So Why Is It Fresh)" by
DST and the Infinity Rappers**

Since "Rockit" hit worldwide fame
The evolution of scratch extremely
changed
This was because of one person with the
master plan
Whose idol and title was the Grand Man
His innovative, cut creative
Sense to manipulate records like an in-
strument
The quality of mink as he mixes in synch
Doin' complicated cuts like it's a cinch
He mixes together different records
For "The Mega Mix"
This is a sample or an example
To witness some of my master tricks
And as you hear it on the radio
Cuts incomparable
No one comes that close
With the peak of the scratch
No one can match
Catch a DST overdose

"The New York City Rap Tour" was a kind of throw-everything-in-the-pot, let's-make-big-money-fast scam cooked up by Bernard Zekri, who was then the New York correspondent for *Actuel* magazine. Conceived when the media were still insisting that rap, graffiti, double-dutch rope jumping, and breakdancing were all part of the same thrilling South Bronx cultural explosion, the tour's bill included Afrika Bambaataa, Fab 5 Freddy, Rammellzee, and Grandmixer DST & the Infinity Rappers (it was DST's scratching that helped to make Herbie Hancock's "Rockit" such a smash the next year). Also aboard were the breakdancing Rock Steady Crew, the Double Dutch Girls, and the graffiti artists Phase 2, Futura, and Dondi. This motley crew, hyped to the skies by several stories in *Actuel,* flew to Paris for the start of their tour in November 1982.

One of the key players in this extravaganza was Fab 5 Freddy. We know him today as the host of the weekend edition of "Yo! MTV Raps," but back then he was known as the young rap promoter/graffiti artist/scenemaker who had helped bring uptown hip-hop to the downtown rockers hanging out at the Roxy (a former roller rink turned hip-hop spot run by English expatriate Cool Lady Blue). Having recently been hailed by name in Blondie's number one pop-rap fantasy, "Rapture," Fred was given the opportunity to make a rap record. It was called "Change the Beat" and released on the Celluloid label. (Nodding to his French patrons, Fred pronounces *change* with a French accent—"shahnge"—throughout the record.) Fred, who is not now, and never was, a rapper, recently reflected on this unusual twist of fate: "I thought it was a cool fuckin' scam. The paintings wasn't movin' too fast. It wasn't like I was fighting to launch a career as a rapper. I was just tryin' to get the rent paid."

The show itself was improvised as the tour progressed. Fred recalls it as "pure b-boyism," and further recalls Futura and Dondi painting huge subway car–size backdrop murals onstage during the show at every stop.

After nine dates in France, the tour invaded London. They did three gigs, with one in particular, at a club called the Venue, standing out in Fred's memory: "That was the show which lit the [rap] spark in niggers over there. All kinds of niggers got on the mike and did damage, while DST and Bam rocked the wheels."

They returned to Paris, "tore shit up," and finally headed back home with all the rent money they'd need for awhile.

Cool Lady Blue. At the Empire Diner, Manhattan, 1983.

18   **Manhattan, 1987.**

grandmaster flash and the furious five

From "The Message," 1982

A child is born with no state of mind
Blind to the ways of mankind
God is smiling on you, but he's frowning, too
Because only God knows what you'll go through
You'll grow in the ghetto living second-rate
And your eyes will sing a song of deep hate
The places you play and where you stay
Looks like one great big alleyway
You'll admire all the number-book takers
Thugs, pimps, pushers, and the big money-makers
Driving big cars, spending twenties and tens
And you wanna grow up to be just like them, hah!
Smugglers, scramblers, burglars, gamblers
Pickpockets, peddlers, even panhandlers
You say, "I'm cool, ha! I'm no fool!"
But you wind up dropping out of high school
Now you're unemployed, all nonvoid
Walking 'round like you're Pretty Boy Floyd
Turned stick-up kid, but look what you done did
Got sent up for a eight-year bid
Now your manhood is took and you're a Maytag
Spend the next two years as a undercover fag
Being used and abused to serve like hell
Till one day you was found hung dead in your cell
It was plain to see that your life was lost
You was cold and your body swung back and forth

But now your eyes sing the sad sad song
Of how you lived so fast and died so young

So don't push me 'cause I'm close to the edge
I'm tryin' not to lose my head
Uh-huh huh huh huh!
It's like a jungle sometimes
It makes me wonder how I keep from going under
Huh! Uh-huh huh huh *huh!*
It's like a jungle sometimes
It makes me wonder how I keep from going under

Grandmaster Flash and the Furious Five were rap's first superstars. Formed by Flash (Joseph Saddler) in the Bronx in 1976 (well before the advent of rap records), the lineup eventually included Cowboy (Keith Wiggins), Melle Mel (Melvin Glover), Kidd Creole (Nathaniel "Danny" Glover, Mel's older brother), Rahiem (Guy Williams), and Mr. Ness (Eddie Morris), who'd later call himself Scorpio.

Dubbed "the Toscanini of the turntables" by *Life* magazine, the Barbados-born Flash invented many of the basic techniques that came to define the art of the hip-hop deejay. "Most deejays at parties would simply play a record all the way to the end, but I was too fidgety to wait," he's explained. "So . . . I would do something to enhance the music." Flash is the auteur of "The Adventures of Grandmaster Flash on the Wheels of Steel" (1981), which remains, some ten years after its waxing, perhaps *the* virtuoso display of hip-hop cutting and scratching.

But the group is probably best known for a series of superpotent message songs cut during 1982 and 1983—"The Message," "White LInes," and "New York, New York"—all of which star Melle Mel. The greatest of these is "The Message," which opened up rap as a medium for serious social commentary and is now widely considered one of the very best rock singles of the decade.

By 1983 rap style was changing, and Flash and the crew took their sudden fall from grace badly. When Flash decided to sue Sugar Hill Records for $5 million in royalties and the right to keep the name of the group for his own use at a new label, the group split down the middle, with Flash, Creole, and Rahiem on one side and Mel, Scorpio, and Cowboy on the other. When the dust cleared Flash was awarded no money and retained nothing but the right to the use of the name "Grandmaster Flash." Mel's next three albums were credited to "Grandmaster Melle Mel and the Furious Five."

In 1987 the original group reunited and cut a new album. "We built a car that was ahead of its time," said the hopeful Flash. "We climb back in and we're back in the race." The reunion album went nowhere.

On September 8, 1989, two weeks short of his twenty-ninth birthday, Cowboy died. According to John Leland in *Newsday,* Flash's very first emcee had spent the previous two years strung out on crack and in and out of jail. "By the time he was twenty-three, Cowboy had seen his career peak and fall into obscurity," Leland noted. "To the industry that he had helped found, he might as well have been dead since 1983." A sad sad song indeed.

At The World, Manhattan, 1987.

kurtis blow

Kurtis Blow was born Kurtis Walker in Harlem in 1959. Present at the creation of rap, he was a teenage b-boy when it was still understood that the *b* stood for breaks, as in breakdancing. A few years later, as a communications major at the City College of New York during the day and a club deejay and emcee at night, he met fellow CCNY student Russell Simmons.

As Kurt's manager, Russ transformed Kool DJ Kurt into Kurtis Blow, "the King of Rap," and won him the first major record label deal ever cut for a rapper (with Mercury). By Christmas of 1979 Kurt was out on wax with "Christmas Rappin'." "The Breaks," his biggest hit (over half a million twelve-inch singles sold), ruled throughout the summer and into the fall of 1980. He later hit with "8 Million Stories," "Basketball," and "If I Ruled the World" (from the soundtrack to *Krush Groove*).

Good-looking and amiable, a maker of party records, Kurt really was almost believable as the King during the first half of the Eighties, when the kingdom of rap comprised an area, metaphorically speaking, about the size of Rhode Island. His star waned as Run-DMC's waxed (a bitterly ironic turn of events for him, given that Run had started out billed as "the Son of Kurtis Blow"), and by the mid-Eighties it was pretty much entirely eclipsed.

From "Rappin' Blow"

I'm Kurtis Blow on the microphone
A place called Harlem was my home
I was rockin' one day, I started to shake
It sounded to me like an earthquake
I packed my bags, I said goodbye
I kissed my woman and started to fly
I came to Earth via meteorite
To rock you all on the mike
So just kick off your shoes, let your fin-
   gers pop
'Cause Kurtis Blow's just about ready to
   rock
Not a preacher or a teacher or a electri-
   cian
A fighter or a writer or a politician
The man with the key to your ignition
Kurtis Blow is competition
Young ladies, shock the house
Yes, young la-*dies,* shock the house
Now just throw your hands in the air
And wave 'em like ya just don't care
If y'all really ready t'rock the house
This morning, somebody say, "Oh, yeah"
(Oh, yeah!)
Somebody scream!
(Ohhhhhh!)
Uh, young ladies
Mercedes
All the ladies in the house say,
   "Owwwww"
("Owwwwww")
Say, "Ho!"
   ("Ho!")
And all the brothers
Fly guys, get high
Say, "Macho!"
("Macho!")
"Macho!"
("Macho!")
"Mucho macho!"

("Mucho macho!")
Keep on rockin' on
Keep keep on rock the hip the hop on
Like a little boy blue blowin' on a horn
The needle on a record tryin' ta play a
   song
It's been that way since the day I was
   born
Like a twenty-five-cent bag of popcorn
Dip dip dab, so-socialize
Clean out your ears and open up your
   eyes
So you here all can realize
That I'm here to tranquilize
Got the knack of Kojak, better than Bar-
   etta
Casanova Brown because I'm down
Uh, get down, stop messin' around
When Kurtis Blow is in your town
I'm a one-of-a-kind, I'll wreck your mind
Put a wiggle, double wiggle, in your be-
   hind
Twice as nice, I'm skatin' on ice
When my momma gave birth she made me
   the baddest
Emcee on earth, y'all
To the beat that makes you free
Get outta your seat and freak to the beat
The weather is cold so catch some heat
(It's ten o'clock! Go to bed!)
(But I don't want to!)

22

With members of the Zulu Nation, the Bronx, 1983.

afrika bambaataa

From "Looking for the Perfect Beat"

**From a different solar system, many many
  galaxies away
We are the force of another creation, a
  new musical revelation
And we're on this musical message to help
  the others listen
In groups from land to land, singin' elec-
  tronic jams**

From "Planet Rock"

**It's time to chase your dreams
Up out your seat, make your body sway
Socialize, get down, let your soul lead
  the way
Shake it, now, go ladies, it's a living
  dream
Love, life, live
Come play the game, our world is free
Just do what you want, but scream!**

Afrika Bambaataa is one of the most widely respected of the elders of hip-hop. Born and raised in the Bronx, Bam was scarcely into his teens when he joined the notorious Black Spades gang. By 1976, when he began throwing his first hip-hop parties, he had formed the Zulu Nation, a gang with a difference: they were dedicated to music, not mayhem. Author Steven Hager, in *Hip Hop: The Illustrated History of Break Dancing, Rap Music, and Graffiti,* has described Bam in action in an early battle of the deejays: "He opened his show with the theme song from 'The Andy Griffith Show,' taped off his TV set. He mixed the ditty with a rocking drum beat, followed it with 'The Munsters' theme song and quickly changed gears with 'I Got the Feeling' by James Brown." The method to Bam's madness? "I played whatever made you rock, no matter what it was."

Turned onto the downtown music scene by Fab 5 Freddy, who hooked Bam up with a gig at the Roxy, Bam shortly began to dream up a musical way to bridge the uptown and downtown scenes. The results on wax were the aptly named "Planet Rock" (1982) and "Looking for the Perfect Beat" (1983). Produced by Arthur Baker and John Robie and cut by Bam with Soul Sonic Force, these records fused funk and hip-hop with the robot trance music of Kraftwerk, sold hundreds of thousands of copies all over the world, and have since taken on the stature of classics.

A one-man ambassador of hip-hop, Bam has gone on to cut records with James Brown, John Lydon (the erstwhile Johnny Rotten), Yellowman, and UB40. His influence endures in the present day in the work of Afrika Islam (the Bam protégé who now produces Ice-T) and the Jungle Brothers (whose chief lyricist and rapper calls himself Afrika Baby Bambaataa in tribute to the original). Indeed, it appears as if, as ever, what goes around, comes around: in June 1990 Bam and the Soul Sonic Force, with support from the Jungle Brothers, released "Return to Planet Rock (The Second Coming)" on Warlock Records.

Manhattan, May 1986.

23

24

Manhattan, 1990.

dr. jeckyll &
mr. hyde

From "Getting Money"

Hey, girl, I'm Dr. Jeckyll
I don't have a care
I'm spendin' money like a millionaire, huh!
I own a mansion and even a yacht
That's right, there ain't a *thing* that I ain't
got
I drive a cherry red Mercedes Benz
I got bank that has no end
I got a Lear Jet at Kennedy
And it's chillin' on the runway layin' for me

Now H-y-d-e
I live a life of luxury
When you see me I'm always fresh
A fly kid and, yes, I'm def
And when I roll up on the scene
I got a chauffeured black limousine
No gray clouds, only sun
I'm gettin' crazy cash money and I'm havin'
big fun

Gettin' money, gettin' money
Everything is funny when you're gettin'
money

Dr. Jeckyll & Mr. Hyde, "the suit-and-tie rappers," had *options.* Either they were going to make it as performers or they'd make it behind the scenes, but one way or another they were going to have careers in the music business. As it turned out, the duo from the Bronx (Andre "Dr. Jeckyll" Harrell and Alonzo "Mr. Hyde" Brown, along with their deejay George "Scratch on Galaxy" Llado), had a decent run as recording artists. They were hardworking and funny and likeable. Their 1981 "Genius Rap" (built on the beat of Tom Tom Club's "Genius of Love") not only sold over 150,000 copies in twelve-inch single form, it single-handedly kept Profile Records from bankruptcy. Their biggest hit was "AM/PM," backed with "Fast Life" (produced for them by Kurtis Blow in 1984), but audience indifference to their first and only album, *The Champagne of Rap* (1986), convinced them that it was time to try something new.

Andre quickly formed Uptown Enterprises. A management firm and record label, Uptown went on to enjoy tremendous success with Heavy D & the Boyz, Al B. Sure!, and the Teddy Riley/Guy posse. Alonzo began a new career doing radio promotion for Cold Chillin' Records, switched over into publicity for Warner Brothers, and is currently head of artists & repertoire for A&M, working with such artists as Janet Jackson, Barry White, and Seduction. The two of them are also working together on Groove B. Chill, a rap act with two emcees and a deejay that, says Alonzo, is "the next Jeckyll & Hyde."

But somehow Andre and Alonzo still can't get the original Jeckyll & Hyde out of their systems. As of this writing the two old friends are threatening to reactivate the old act.

Gettin' money, so much money, girl
Everything is funny when you're gettin'
money
One million
Two million
Three million
Four!
Five million
Six million
Seven million
More!
One billion
Two billion
Three billion
Four!
Five billion
Six billion
Seven billion
More!

25

26

Manhattan, 1983.

the fearless four

From "Problems of the World Today"

Daddy, we had fun the weekend that just
    passed
Mommy's brother came to visit while you
    were away
I know why you look puzzled; I was
    shocked myself
I didn't know I had an uncle until Friday
I was really glad I met him, but places
    Mommy pet him
Brought them both some ugly faces, so
    they went in the back
Thought it was kinda crazy, but I know as
    a fact
There's no way in the world I'd kiss my sis-
    ter like that
What do you mean she has no brother? I
    saw him myself
And we can go check with Mother just to
    see what she'll say
Thought you would be glad to know I had
    an uncle
Didn't know you'd come home and beat
    my mommy that way

Problems
Problems
Problems
Problems of the world today

The Fearless Four, in full effect, were really the Fearless Six—four emcees and two deejays. The emcees were the Great Peso (Mitchell Grant), the Devastating Tito (Tito Dones, who rapped in English and Spanish), Mighty Mike C (Michael Kevin Clee), and DLB, the Microphone Wizard. The deejays were O.C. (Oscar Rodriguez, Jr.) and Krazy Eddie (Eddie Thompson). They racked up two notable early rap hits: "Rockin' It," on Bobby Robinson's Enjoy label in 1981, and "Problems of the World Today," which Kurtis Blow produced for Elektra in 1983. They made records for a while afterward, but had no more hits.

The following autobiographical statements, from the Elektra bio current at the time of "Problems of the World Today," continue to provide a window onto the fascinating and amusing particulars of b-boy style, circa 1983.

The Great Peso "I was born under Sagittarius, December 5, 1959. Color? I can make anything stand out. I like Whoppers, fried chicken, fish, corn. I like to go out to discos, see five movies in a weekend. On girls: I like to have a few. My personality changes like the weather."

Mighty Mike C "I'm Pisces, born March 10, 1963. My favorite color is sky blue. I like pretty girls. My girls. I like Krazy Eddie's girls. I like to have fun. I like home cooking—my mother's cooking, and DLB's grandmother's. I like to drink champagne and watch TV."

The Devastating Tito "I'm Gemini, May 27, 1964. Favorite color is black. Food: sirloin steak. My favorite kind of girl will stay unspoken. I like to go to Broadway plays every now and then. I also like roller skating and dancing."

O.C. "I'm a Virgo. Birthdate: September 22, 1962. I like spinning records, producing records, making music and having fun. I'm from Manhattan. My favorite color: blue. Favorite kind of woman: blond hair, blue eyes. Food: lasagna and shrimp."

Krazy Eddie "I'm a Leo, born July 25, 1960. I have two beautiful kids, twin daughter and son, seven months old. I like playing basketball, swimming, fishing, roller skating, drawing. Food: collard greens, steaks, ribs. My favorite color is a beige brown. Woman: a healthy woman."

DLB, the Microphone Wizard "I'm a Taurus, born April 25. I do not reveal my name, birth, or my age. I am the youngest member of the group, though. Color: black, the mysterious color. I could eat steak for breakfast. I like a girl who is devoted to the fullest . . . and truthful to the same extent. I like to draw, I like to sing and write lyrics. I love kung-fu pictures. I'm like a slave to my art. Most of all, in my spare time, I'm a lovemaker. I love to make love. My black suit turns red at night."

Hollis, Queens, 1984.

run-dmc

Now Peter Piper picked peppers, but Run
rocked rhymes

Humpty Dumpty fell down, that's his hard
time

Jack B. Nimble was nimble and he was
quick

But Jam Master's much faster, Jack's on
Jay's dick

Now Little Bo Peep cold lost her sheep

And Rip Van Winkle fell the hell asleep

And Alice chillin' somewhere in Wonder-
land

Jack servin' Jill, bucket in his hand

"Is Jam Master Jay flakin'?!" How that
sound?

The turntables might wobble, but they
don't fall down

. . . Jay's like King Midas, as I was told

Everything that he touched turned to gold

He's the greatest of the greater, get it
straight, he's great

Claims fame 'cause his name is known in
every state

His name is Jay, to see him play will make
you say:

"Goddamn, that deejay made my day!"

. . . Tricks are for kids, he plays much gigs

He's the Big Bad Wolf and you're the
Three Pigs

He's the Big Bad Wolf in your neighbor-
hood

Not "bad" meaning bad, but bad meaning
good!

. . . We're Run-DMC got a beef to settle

D's not Hansel, [Run's] not Gretel

Jay's a winner, not a beginner

His pockets get fat, others' get thinner

Jump on Jay like cows jump moons

People chase Jay like dish and spoon

And like all fairytales end

You'll see Jay again, my friend

Run-DMC was rap's breakthrough crew, the one that, in DMC's words, "took the beat from the street and put it on TV." Comprising Run (Joseph Simmons), DMC (Darryl McDaniels), and Jam Master Jay (Jason Mizell), Run-DMC hailed from Hollis, Queens, a black working-class-to-middle-class community several steps up the economic ladder from the South Bronx. Their relatively elevated living conditions provided them with a relatively elevated perspective; unlike Melle Mel and the Furious Five, Run and D saw more of life than "rats in the front room / roaches in the back / junkies in the alley with a baseball bat."

Ironically, their work (and their everyday b-boy gear) was much more down-to-earth . . . and much more hard-core. They were certainly not the first b-boys, but they were the first to make b-boy records. (As a result, they incidentally killed off the careers of the entire generation of rappers—Furious Five, Fearless Four, Treacherous Three, and so on—who now think of themselves as members of the old school.) They were also the first rappers to have a gold album, the first to have a platinum album, the first to have a double-platinum album, the first on "American Bandstand," the first on MTV, the first to win an endorsement contract from a sportswear manufacturer, the first to perform on Ivy League college campuses, the first on the cover of *Rolling Stone,* and the only rappers at Live Aid.

Their trio of early "rap-rock" records—"Rock Box" (1984), "King of Rock" (1985), and "Walk This Way" (cut with Aerosmith, 1986)—were tremendously influential in convincing music lovers of all stripes that rap *is* rock, and that it consequently shouldn't be ghetto-ized. They've always had a lot of fun, but they've also always willingly acted as role models for the black community.

After having virtually defined rap between 1983 and 1987, it became fashionable in rap circles to try to knock Run-DMC off their perch. By 1989 the crew's hard-core stance had become such a cliché that De La Soul, in songs like "Me, Myself, & I," was able to fashion a new, loose, playful style more or less in direct opposition to it. As of this writing, old friends and fans (including this writer) are anxiously awaiting the release of Run-DMC's fifth album.

29

Manhattan, 1988.

Manhattan, 1988. (Human Beat Box, inset.)

30

the fat boys

From "Fat Boys"

Prince Markie Dee!
Kool Rock-ski!
The Human Beat Box providing the beat!
One thousand pounds put all together
The Disco Brothers to last forever
And when we enter a room the ground
    starts quakin'
The crowd starts breakin' and the bodies
    start shakin'
To the funky rhythm, to the beat called
    Fats
So bust the fresh move—individual raps

Now I'm Markie D, but you can call me the
    Prince
I had a slight problem that I couldn't
    solve since
I was a boy. Yeah, I over-ate at a steady
    pace rate
Yeah, I'm overweight
. . . Now it started off when I was very
    small
I devoured chocolate cakes: plates, can-
    dles and all
For breakfast it was cheese and five
    pounds of bacon
And halfway through my tummy starts to
    shakin'
Toast on the side, five gallons of juice
And that was just for breakfast when I
    start to get loose

Well, my name is Kool Rock, the last part
    is Ski
And I'm the captain rocker of the Disco
    Three
I got pizzazz, style, and grace
Just one slight problem: I'm a little over-
    weight
But my walk is funky, my style hip-hop

Every time I touch a girl, they always yell,
    "Stop!"
'Cause around my block I'm king of the
    slop
But I know one thing: my heart keeps its
    spot
It says do the right thing and you will sur-
    vive
People still put me down 'cause I'm the
    mess of the town
But I got one thing that's hard to beat
    and that's class
Yeah, that's right, ladies!
I'm a little overweight but I'll pass, huh
I'm like glass
Yes, I'm easy to break
And if you get me wrong, that's a chance
    you take
Yes, my word is bond and that's no mis-
    take
. . . The beat called fats will rock the spot
So party people rock on to the Human
    Beat Box . . .

The Fat Boys—heavy before Heavy D & the Boyz and "lite" before Salt 'n' Pepa and Kid 'n' Play—were rap's first frankly pop act. They remade "Wipeout" with backing vocals by the Beach Boys. They remade "The Twist" with Chubby Checker. They starred in a movie called *Disorderlies* with Ralph Bellamy and Anthony Geary. They made a cameo appearance on an episode of "Miami Vice," starred in a couple of very slick and funny TV commercials for Swatch Watch, and released the world's first rap opera. They sold millions of records and they worked their huge asses off, touring nonstop, nationally and internationally, for six years.

But well before they were hailed as "natural comedians" and packaged as a blimpish cartoon, they were three relatively earnest teenage rap fiends—Mark "Prince Markie Dee" Morales, Damon "Kool Rock-ski" Wimbley, and Darren Robinson, "the Human Beat Box"—from the same rough neighborhood in East New York, Brooklyn. Competing as the Disco Three, they won a citywide talent contest at Radio City Music Hall in 1983. First prize included a recording contract, but even more important was the hook-up with wily Swiss-born manager Charles Stettler. Presented with a hotel bill for $350 in "extra breakfasts" on an early European tour with the trio, it was Stettler who suggested that they really ought to change their name to the Fat Boys. The next single, entitled, "Fat Boys," was a hit, and the single after that was *by* the Fat Boys, and after that there was no looking back.

They seem to have dropped off the scene the past couple of years, but the Fat Boys may yet be back with us. In a recent newspaper story about the Fat Boys' $6 million suit against their old record label, Markie Dee made the following announcement in passing: "We're gonna lose some weight, call ourselves the Hefty Posse, and start fresh for the Nineties."

31

full force

Full Force is included in this book for two reasons: (1) They have been cast as cartoon thugs in two of the more notable "rap movies" (*Krush Groove,* 1985, starring Run-DMC and the Fat Boys, and *House Party,* 1990, starring Kid 'n' Play); and (2) We love this picture. Strictly speaking, Full Force is not a rap crew. They are a hip-hop–influenced R & B band and a self-contained production team (notably responsible for UTFO's "Roxanne, Roxanne," and for albums by Lisa Lisa & Cult Jam, Cheryl "Pepsii" Riley, the Real Roxanne, and James Brown, among others).

Janette got this picture after having shot group photos of Full Force on the roof of a building in midtown Manhattan for a profile in *The Face.* Impressed by the fellas' pumped-up physiques, Janette then wondered if she couldn't take shots of the crew's individual, uh, *members.* "Show me your body," she said to Paul Anthony, who obliged by dropping trou and striking the pose immortalized here.

Manhattan, 1986.

33

Left: **Paul Anthony. Manhattan, 1986.**

Roxanne Shante. At "Rapmania," Manhattan, 1990.

the "roxanne, roxanne" syndrome (utfo/roxanne shante/ the real roxanne)

"Roxanne, Roxanne" was more than a record and a dozen or so answer records. It was a phenomenon, a wild public debate about then-current teen sexual etiquette, and it deserves a whole little chapter of its own in the history of rap.

It started out as a great record by UTFO, a four-man crew from East Flatbush, Brooklyn, two of whom—Dr. Ice and the Kangol Kid—were then touring as Whodini's breakdancers. A Full Force production built on the slammin' drum track from Billy Squier's "The Big Beat," "Roxanne, Roxanne" told the story of a young ghetto princess who has all the attitude she needs to reject the successive come-ons of the three rappers in the group.

It immediately inspired a vicious answer record from a real-life fourteen-year-old from the Queensbridge Projects in Long Island City named Lolita Shante Gooden—a big fan of Millie Jackson—who not only wrote and rapped "Roxanne's Revenge" but reinvented herself as Roxanne Shante. Hot on her heels were the Real Roxanne (produced by Full Force), the Original Roxanne, and Sparky D, all of whom staked out different positions in the controversy. Roxanne was a feminist, a snob, or a slut. UTFO were sex-crazed creeps, losers, or the innocent victims of an unprovoked attack.

New voices were heard from and new theories advanced on a weekly basis: "Roxanne's a Virgin," "Roxanne's a Man," "Roxanne's Little Sister," "Ice Roxanne," and "Roxanne's Doctor." It was clear that the fever had finally burned itself out when "No More Roxanne, Please" surfaced.

Looking back on it in 1989, Shante told *Soul Underground*'s Malu Halasa: "Oh, God! They played it on the radio so much, I just turned the radio off. That's the attitude I took. Mind you, I was only fourteen. I couldn't go to school no more because of my popularity. People came and stood outside my class. The teachers thought it would be best if I got a tutor because they said my presence was disrupting. My mom was shocked. My dad was shocked. My mom said, 'We're rich!' and we were. I turned fifteen and I bought my first Cadillac. I bought it because I was little and I wanted the best car, and I didn't know about Mercedes Benz back then, so I got a Fleetwood.

"I wanted to be a lawyer. That was my main goal. All of this happened by accident. I wanted to prove a point to someone."

The Real Roxanne (back row, fourth from left). Brooklyn, 1986.

From "Roxanne, Roxanne" by UTFO

Yo, EMD
Yeah, what's up, man?
There go that girl they call Roxanne.
  She's all stuck up.
Why do you say that?
'Cause she wouldn't give a guy like me
  no rap.

Man, she was walkin' down the street
  so I said, "Hello,
I'm Kangol from UTFO"
She said, "So?" I said, "So?!"
Baby, don't you know?
I can sing, rap, dance in just one show
'Cause I'm Kangol, Mr. Sophisticator
Star sign, no, ain't nobody greater
From beginning to end, end to begin-
  ning
I never lose 'cause I'm all about win-
  ning"

. . . I thought she'd be impressed and
  give me devious rap
I thought I had her caught inside my
  sinister trap
I thought it'd be a piece of cake, but
  it was nothin' like that
I guess that's what I get for thinkin',
  ain't that right, black?

. . . Brother, I feel bad
But I ain't committing suicide with no
  crab
Calling her a crab is just a figure of
  speech
'Cause she's a apple, a pear, a plum,
  and a peach
I thought I had her in the palm of my
  hand
But man, oh man, if I was grand I'd
  bang Roxanne, Roxanne

Roxanne, Roxanne
Can't you understand
Roxanne, Roxanne
I wanna be your man

36

Yo, Kangol, I don't think that you're
  dense
But you went about the matter with no
  experience
You should know: she doesn't need a
  guy like you
She needs a guy like me with a high
  I.Q.

And she'll take to my rap 'cause my
  rap's the best
The Educated Rapper, M.D., will never
  'fess
So when I met her I wasted no time
But stuck-up Roxanne paid me no mind
". . . It's only customary to give this
  commentary
Some say it's rap, some say it's leg-
  endary
You're searchin' all you want and try
  your local library
You'll never find a rhyme like this in
  any dictionary."
But do you know after all that
All I received was a pat on the back
That's what you get. It happened to
  me
Ain't that right, Mix Master I-c-e?

Roxanne, Roxanne
Roxanne, Roxanne

You thought you had her roped, you
  thought you was Cupid
But, EMD, your rap was plain stupid
I know you're educated, but when will
  you learn?
Not all girls want to be involved with
  bookworms
You gotta be strong in ways she can't
  resist
Now Educated Rapper, huh, bust this:
Since she's the new girl around the
  block
I had to let her know I was the debon-
  air Doc
I said, "I'd like to speak with you, if I
  can
And if I'm correct, then your name is
  Roxanne."
She said, "How'd you know my name?"
I said, "It's gettin' around.
Right now, baby, you're the talk of the
  town.
Please let me walk you to the corner,
  my rap will be brief."
She said, "I seen you before. You look
  like a thief."
I said, "Me? The Doc? A hood? A rock?
Runnin' 'round the street, robbin' peo-
ple on the block?
Naaah . . . that's not my style, to
  crime I'm not related
As far as I'm concerned, I'm too so-
  phisticated."

Then it seemed I got through, 'cause
  she cracked a smile
That let me know my rap was worth her
  while

. . . She said, "Ooooh! That's very
  unique!"
Gave me her number and kissed me on
  the cheek
She said she had to go, but she'd be
  back by eight
Told me call her at nine to arrange a
  date
"Did you take her to the beach?"
"That's what we planned. But she
  stood me up, Roxanne,
Roxanne . . ."

**From "Roxanne's Revenge" by Roxanne
  Shante**

I met these three guys and you know
  it's true
Let me tell you and explain them all to
  you
I met this dude with the name of a hat
I didn't even walk away, I didn't give
  him no rap
But then he got real mad and he got a
  little tired
If he worked for me, you know he
  would be fired
He wears a Kangol and that is cute
But he ain't got the money and he ain't
  got the loot
Every time that I see him he says a
  rhyme
You see compared to me, it's weak
  compared to mine

. . . After that there was the Educated
  Rapper
His fingers start to snap-a and my
  hands start to clap-a
. . . He should be like me, a fly emcee
Don't never have to bite, will always
  write
I have the freshest rhymes that I do re-
  cite

. . . But let me tell you somethin' else
  about the Doctor, too
He ain't really cute and he ain't great
He don't even know how to operate

UTFO: The Kangol Kid, Mixmaster Ice, and Dr. Ice. Brooklyn, 1986.

He came up to me with some crab-ish
    rap
But lemme tell you somethin': don't
    you know it was wack

. . . I turned you down, without a
    frown
Embarrassed you in front of your
    friends, made you look like a clown
And all you do is get real mad
And you talk about me and make *me*
    look bad?!
But everybody knows how the story
    goes

There's no ifs, no ands, no buts or
    suppose
No coke up your nose, no dope in
    your vein
And then it won't cause no kind of
    pain
But yet and still you're tryin' to be fly
I asked you a question. I wanna know
    why
Why'd you have to make a record 'bout
    me?
The R-o-x-a-n-n-e

Lyrics by L. Gooden. Copyright © 1984 by Marlon Williams

From "The Real Roxanne" by the Real
    Roxanne

. . . me, the Rox, give up the box?
So you can brag about it for the next
    six blocks?
Where's the beef? You guys can't deal
    it
I need a man who can make me feel it

Copyright © 1984 by Full Force

38

Manhattan, 1990.

slick rick

From "Children's Story"

Once upon a time not long ago
When people wore pajamas and lived life
   slow
When laws were stern and justice stood
And people were behavin' like they ought
   to: good
There lived a little boy who was misled
By another little boy and this is what he
   said:
"Me and you, Ty, we're gonna make some
   cash
Robbin' old folks and making the dash"
They did the job, money came with ease
But one couldn't stop. It's like he had a
   disease
He robbed another and another and a sis-
   ter and her brother
Tried to rob a man who was a Dt. under-
   cover
The cop grabbed his arm, he started act-
   ing erratic
He said, "Keep still, boy, no need for
   static"
Punched him in his belly and he gave him
   a slap
But little did he know the little boy was
   strapped
The kid pulled out a gun. He said, "Why'd
   you hit me?"
The barrel was set straight for the cop's
   kidney
The cop got scared. The kid, he starts to
   figure:
"I'll get years if I pull this trigger."
So he cold dashed and ran around the
   block
Cop radios in to another lady cop
He ran by a tree, there he saw this sister.
Shot for the head. He shot back and
   missed her
Looked 'round good and from expecta-
   tions
He decided he'd head for the subway sta-
   tions
But she was comin' and he made a
   left

He was runnin' top speed till he was
   out of breath
Knocked an old man down and swore
   he killed 'im
Then he made his move to an aban-
   doned buildin'
Ran up the stairs, up to the top floor
Opened up a door there. Guess who
   he saw?
Dave, the dope fiend, shootin' dope
Who don't know the meanin' of water
   nor soap
He said, "I need bullets! Hurry up!
   Run!"
The dope fiend brought back a span-
   kin' shotgun
He went outside but there was cops
   all over
Then he dipped into a car, a stolen
   Nova
Raced up the block doin' eighty-
   three
Crashed into a tree near University
Escaped alive, though the car was
   battered
Rat-a-tat-tatted and all the cops
   scattered
Ran out of bullets and he still had
   static
Grabbed a pregnant lady and pulled
   out the automatic

Pointed at her head, he said the gun
   was full of lead
He told the cops, "Back off, or
   honey here's dead!"
Deep in his heart he knew he was
   wrong
So he let the lady go and he starts
   to run on
Sirens sounded, he seemed as-
   tounded
And before long the little boy got
   surrounded
He dropped the gun. So went the
   glory
And this is the way I must end this
   story:
He was only seventeen, in a mad-
   man's dream
The cops shot the kid. I still hear him
   scream
This ain't funny, so don't you dare
   laugh
Just another case about the wrong
   path
Straight and narrow, or your soul
   gets cast
Good night!

Slick Rick is one of rap's more elusive and controversial figures. He made a sensational debut as MC Ricky D on Doug E. Fresh's "The Show" and "La-Di-Da-Di" in 1985 and then disappeared for three full years. He returned with "The Great Adventures of Slick Rick" in 1988 to the platinum embrace of his American fans . . . and a virtual banning by English music critics, who were so offended by what they took to be his misogyny that they didn't even bother to condemn the album—they simply didn't write about it at all. Though his work is very definitely adults-only, we celebrate his wild sense of humor, his cheerful smut-tiness, his eye for detail, his ear for dialogue, his talent for structuring a song-length narrative, and his commitment to telling the tales of the ghetto.

Born Ricky Walters to Jamaican parents in South Wimbledon, London, and raised there for most of his first fourteen years, Rick comes by his posh English accent honestly. His hip-hop sensibility, on the other hand, was formed in the North Bronx, which is where he and his family moved from London and where he still lives. A painstaking writer and producer, Slick Rick was at work on his second album as of this writing.

40

Manhattan, 1986.

doug e. fresh

From "The Show"

Well, it started off on Eighth Avenue
When I made up a name called the Get
   Fresh Crew
It was me, my two deejays, Chill Will and
   Barry Bee
And my right-hand man Ricky D.
I used to rap and sing, make sounds and
   things
(Dr-r-r-r-ring! Dr-r-r-r-ring!)
"Hello, is Doug E. Fresh in?"
"No, he's not in right now"
(Click-ick!)
But anyway, no more delay
Just check out the new style I display
Now you gotta be fresh
To rock with Fresh
And I'm D-o-u-g-i-e Fresh
The Human Beat Box, or the Entertainer
No other title can fit me plainer
In a passing generation I am a remainer
And I'm also known as the Beat Box
   Trainer
Cashin' checks, make sound effects
And after I finish rockin', Slick Rick is on
   next

Doug E. Fresh is living proof that—in rap at least—nice guys often finish second. Born Douglas Davis on St. Thomas, the Virgin Islands, Doug grew up in Brooklyn, the Bronx, and Harlem. Though he'd pioneered the arsenal of techniques that earned him the right to bill himself as the Original Human Beat Box—a repertoire of clicks, oinks, pops, bird calls, silly voices, and other sound effects—Doug didn't make it onto record until *after* Darren Robinson, the Fat Boys' Human Beat Box, whose own debut had made a considerable splash. (He may have taken some small consolation in the fact that by 1986 the Oberheim Emulator had a "Doug E. Fresh" chip, which mimicked the sound of Doug in his Human Beat Box mode.)

Even more frustrating, the biggest hits of Doug's career—"The Show," backed with "La-Di-Da-Di"—featured his "right-hand man," the nasty Mr. Slick Rick, who did not long remain a member of Doug's crew and who, as a solo artist, has gone on to achieve considerably more success than Doug.

In 1986 Doug told *Spin*'s John Leland: "It's a gift for a person to be able to sit back and think of things and draw the attention of the whole population and just make them feel good . . . and it only happens to those that can handle that type of responsibility. I don't indulge in no type of get high: I don't drink, don't smoke, don't sniff. I don't even eat meat. The only thing I do is hang out sometimes."

With Chill Will, left, and Barry Bee, right. Manhattan, 1986.

42

With hickey. Manhattan, 1987.

ll cool j

LL Cool J is one of the few rappers in the history of the music capable of expressing extreme b-boy aggression *and* blazing sex-god passion—a range noted by such disparate arbiters of taste as *The New York Times,* which claimed in 1986 that then-eighteen-year-old LL radiated "the charisma of the young Muhammad Ali"; the editors of *Playgirl,* who named him to their list of the Ten Sexiest Men in Rock 'n' Roll in 1988; the law enforcement czars of Columbus, Georgia, who arrested him for "public lewdness" after a show there in 1987; and First Lady Nancy Reagan, who asked him to headline a "Just Say No" concert for her at Radio City Music Hall half a year later.

LL was hailed as a major hero of hip-hop virtually from the moment he began recording as a sixteen-year-old prodigy in 1984, although his career really got a boost from his performance of "I Can't Live Without My Radio" in *Krush Groove* in 1985, a ninety-second cameo that pretty much stole the movie from Run-DMC, Shiela E, the Fat Boys, and Blair Underwood. His "I Need Love" was the first rap single ever to reach the top of *Billboard's* Hot Black Singles chart, and all three of his albums have gone platinum or better.

Born James Todd Smith in St. Albans, Queens, in January 1968, an only child, LL is very much a *solo* rapper. He once told England's *Record Mirror:* "When I die, bury me on my stomach and let the world kiss my ass."

From "Rock the Bells"

The bells are scintillatin' like the blood in
  your veins
Why are girlies on the tip?
(LL's your name!)
Cut Creator's good
Cool J's good-good
You bring the woodpecker, I'll bring the
  wood
The bells are whippin' and rippin' at your
  body and soul
Why do you like Cool J?
We like rock 'n' roll!
'Cause it ain't the glory days with Bruce
  Springsteen
I'm not a virgin so I know I'll make Ma-
  donna scream
You hated Michael and Prince all the way
  ever since
If their beats were made of meat then
  they would have to be mince
Rock the bells!

All you gonna-be wannabees when will
  you learn?
Wanna be like Cool J, you gotta wait your
  turn
Some suckers don't like me, but I'm not
  concerned
Six g's for twenty minutes is the pay I earn
I'm growin' and glowin' like a forest blaze
Do you like Michael Jackson?
(We like Cool J!)
That's right, I'm on the mike with the help
  of the bells
And no delayin' what I'm sayin' 'cause I'm
  rockin' you well
Rock the bells!

43

With Cut Creator, left, E Love, third from left, B-Rock, far right. Manhattan, 1987.

44

MCA, Ad-Rock, and Mike D. Manhattan, 1985.

the beastie boys

From "Hold It Now—Hit It!"

Emcee Adam Yauch in the place to be
Ah, the girls are on me 'cause I'm down
   with Mike D
I'm down with Mike D and it ain't no ba-
   loney
For real, not phony—O.E. and Rice-a-Roni
I come out at night 'cause I sleep all day
Well, I'm the King Adrock and he's MCA
Well, I'm cruisin', I'm bruisin', I'm never
   ever losin'
I'm in my car, I'm goin' far, and dust is
   what I'm usin'
Around the way is where I'm from
And I'm from Manhattan and I'm not a bum
Because you're a pud-slappin', ball-flap-
   pin', got that juice
My name's Mike D and I can do that Jerry
   Lewis

Hip-hoppin', body rockin', doin' the do
Beer drinkin', breath stinkin', sniffin' glue
Belly fillin', always illin', bustin' caps
My name's Mike D and I write my own
   snaps

I'm a peek-show seeking on the Forty-
   Deuce
I'm a killer at large and I'm on the loose
Pistol-packin', Monkey-drinkin', no-money
   bum
I come from Brooklyn 'cause that's where
   I'm from

Cheapskate, perpetratin', money-hungry
   jerk
Every day I drink O.E. and I don't go to
   work
You drippy-nose knucklehead, you're wet
   behind the ears
You like men and we like beer

King of the Ave with the def female
You're rhymin' and stealin' with the fresh-
   est ale

The Beasties Boys screaming "You've got to fight! For your right! To paaaaaar-
ty!" was just what young America needed to hear in 1987. Almost overnight
they'd won it all: the respect and affection of black rap fans and white rockers
alike; the praise of the rock critics and the condemnation of the squares on
the city desk; movie offers and movie-star girlfriends; deals for product en-
dorsements and lawsuits for copyright infringement. They were decried as mon-
sters of pornography by the pillars of a dozen communities and hailed as the
moment's preeminent teen idols by the editors of every rock fanzine in existence.
They blazed through a year that started out like the sweet dream of rock
stardom immortalized in *A Hard Day's Night* and ended in a haze of bad faith
reminiscent of *The Great Rock 'n' Roll Swindle*—even if quadruple-platinum
Licensed to Ill did become the biggest-selling rap album of all time.

Indeed, it was the kind of year that had destroyed the Sex Pistols a decade
earlier. The Beasties—the King Adrock (Adam Horovitz), MCA (Adam Yauch),
and Mike D (Michael Diamond)—survived only by going into hibernation for
two years. When they emerged, with *Paul's Boutique* in the summer of 1989, it
was from a new city (L.A., not New York), with new management and new
producers on a new label . . . and with their old senses of humor and daring
intact. To their credit, the Beasties had not played it safe (there was no "Fight
for Your Right to Party, Round 2"), but something just didn't click this time.
Undaunted, they went back to the drawing board.

Still, whatever the future holds for them, the Beasties will be forever crowned
with laurel in the rock 'n' roll hall of fame. At precisely the moment that Ronald
Reagan's icy death grip on American culture was weakening, the Beastie Boys
hastened the process by throw-
ing a pie in his face. A grateful
nation weeps at the memory.

Coolin' at the crib watchin' my TV
Ed Norton, Ted Knight, and Mr. E-d
Pump it up, homeboy, just don't stop
Chef Boy-Ar-Dee coolin' on the pot
I take no slack 'cause I got the knack
And I'm never dustin' out 'cause I torch
   that crack
The King Adrock, that is my name
You're drinking' Moët, and we got the
   champagne
A quarter-droppin', goin' shoppin', buyin'
   wigs
Surgeon General Cut Professor DJ Thigs!

45

46

Rick Rubin. Manhattan, 1985. Russell Simmons (inset). Manhattan, 1987.

russell simmons and rick rubin

Russell Simmons and Rick Rubin, the pepper-and-salt founders of Def Jam Recordings, may have ultimately been more important in the "greening" of rap than any single recording act in its history. Convinced of the music's built-in beauty and power, disdainful of the pop music (both black and white) of the day, their aim was to help build the careers of artists who would not have to dilute their music in order to cross over to the vast pop audience, but who would instead divert the entire mainstream of pop in their direction. In short, their bold attitude was, "Let them come to us."

Unlike most other music businessmen, Russ and Rick (twenty-seven and twenty-two, respectively, when they formed the label in 1984) were deeply involved in the creative affairs of their artists. Not only was Russ managing the careers of Run-DMC, Whodini, Kurtis Blow, and Dr. Jeckyll & Mr. Hyde, but he had also coproduced (with Larry Smith) Run-DMC's first two albums. Rick had produced T. LaRock and Jazzy Jay's "It's Yours," an instant b-boy classic. Together Rick and Russ coproduced Run-DMC's triple-platinum *Raising Hell*. When it came to LL Cool J and the Beastie Boys, they divided the labor: Rick produced LL's platinum debut album *(Radio)* and the Beasties' quadruple-platinum debut album *(Licensed to Ill)*, while Russ managed the groups. Likewise, when it came to their last joint project, the movie *Tougher Than Leather*, Russ produced and Rick directed.

Sometimes, however, they disagreed: Rick signed Public Enemy to Def Jam over Russ's objections, although Russell did eventually manage their career.

By late 1986 the partnership had soured, and by late 1987 it was all over but for the maneuverings of their respective lawyers. Since then, each guy has reverted to the music of his youth. Russ has devoted a lot of his energy to R & B artists like Alyson Williams, Oran "Juice" Jones, Chuck Stanley, Tashan, Newkirk, Blue Magic, and the Black Flames, although he's also backed custom labels run by Jam Master Jay, Chuck D of Public Enemy, and Ed Lover of "Yo! MTV Raps." Rick has gone on to form the Def American label and to produce such white masters of outrage as Andrew Dice Clay and Slayer (although he was recently moved to produce the Geto Boys, a rap act which he praises as "the most offensive group I've ever worked with.")

The "lyrics" reproduced on this page are excerpted from Russell Simmons's free-form rant on a Jazzy Jay record produced for Def Jam by Rick Rubin early in 1985. The "Doctor" referred to is Andre "Dr. Jeckyll" Harrell, who was in the studio the night the recording was made.

finest Caps and Hats

48

Left to right: **Prince Paul, Delite, Fruitkwan, and Wise.** *In front:* **Daddy-O and DBC. Brooklyn, 1988.**

stetsasonic

From "A.F.R.I.C.A."

I've seen the TV report and I watched it all
week
That Samora Machel of Mozambique
Was killed in a crash that couldn't be ex-
plained
Yo, D, I wanna break!
Yo, brother, refrain!
Kenneth Kaunda's in Zambia, I'm in Amer-
ica
SWAPO's in Namibia, Nyerere's in Tanza-
nia.
Mugabe's in Harare, Jesse just came back
From the homeland, the green and the
black!
So let's spell it out:

A.F.R.I.C.A.
Angola, Soweto, Zimbabwe
Tanzania, Zambia, Mozambique
And Botwsana
So let us speak
About the Motherland

South Africa no free, neither are we
Those are our brothers and sisters across
the sea
I'm speaking for the Stet and we make a
plea
To fight apartheid, everybody
To fight against de wicked and help Mu-
gabe
To fight apartheid and assist Nyerere
Support the MK and the ANC
We wanna see Nelson and Winnie free
You don't know, you need to study
And when you do, we're sure you'll agree
They need help, but so do we
Them with their government
Us with mentality

Stetsasonic (to paraphrase Roxanne Shante on the subject of the Kangol Kid) are some dudes with the name of a hat—a Stetson hat, to be precise. Stetson was the brand they all sported when the six-man crew from Brooklyn's tough Bedford-Stuyvesant neighborhood first came together in 1981. They started recording in 1985, and likely made their biggest splash to date in 1987 with "A.F.R.I.C.A.," a message record about the political situation in southern Africa and what that might have to do with African American kids, the proceeds of which went to the Africa Fund for humanitarian relief projects for the people of the frontline states. It also inspired a great video and an eighteen-page teaching guide designed to teach American high schoolers what was "behind the words" of the song.

Recalling his youth, group leader Daddy-O has said, "We were not the kind of guys who had their milk money stolen. We're street kids, but we see ourselves in a leadership role in the community." Adds Delite, his partner: "We're just a practical posse off the block that's got their shit together."

Brooklyn, 1988.

49

50

justice

From "Kickin' Some Flavor"

Come on and get loose, the mike is like a
noose
It bombs like napalm and harms like death
juice
So drink it and think it, ya blink, ya wink
it or sink it
For the know-how right now to Sun and to
Pow Wow
Homeboys to the end, to the brothers
once again
I don't have no friends 'cause they'll stick
ya like a pin
Like a snake in the grass, stab ya right in
the back
Ya slithering no good, 'cause ya weak and
ya wack
If ya let the person do it, they'll do it
with vigor
Dis ya bad, like an idiot or an ignorant —
——
So get bigger and better, don't let up or
let 'em
Play ya out like cards. If you let 'em,
they'll get ya
Keep this thing alive, let me do ya a favor
Clear my throat, catch my breath, and I'm
gonna kick some more flavor

Justice has made some def records, but he's likely achieved his greatest notoriety to date as the subject of a controversial *Washington Post Magazine* cover story in September of 1986. Entitled "Murder, Drugs and the Rap Star," it detailed the case against him for the murder of a D.C. drug dealer. Trouble was, the case rested on the testimony of a single witness, "a thief and a drug dealer . . . whose own mother would not let him live at home because of his addiction to drugs and wont to steal." Justice himself, of course, denied everything. "This whole thing makes me laugh," he said. "This whole damned thing, every bit of it, is a joke. I'm innocent, man. I didn't do nothin'."

In fact, the case came to just that: absolutely nothing. Justice had been held, but he was never even charged. Finally, there *was* no case to dismiss. But the damage had been done: the local black community understood the story as a smokescreened attack on black youth, and were so pissed off that they picketed on the premises of the paper for several months. (In its own way, the *Post* story was a kind of D.C. precursor of *Newsweek's* "Rap Rage" hatchet job in 1990.)

None of this slowed down the young rapper from Ft. Greene, Brooklyn, born Joseph Williams, Jr., aka Justice, aka Sir Vicious, aka The Original Gangster of Hip-Hop. Looking to the future, he said, "All that's got to happen is they put my face on an album cover and the women'll be chasing me. These women want to be around me for sex. I get tired of that. You do it too much and it makes you skinny."

Janette shot this photo for an album cover. Last time we checked, we heard that Justice was down to 130 pounds.

kid 'n' play

Kid 'n' Play (Christopher Reid and Christopher Martin) established themselves in 1988 and 1989 with a series of polished party songs and an accompanying series of good-looking videos . . . and then broke big in 1990 as the stars of the movie *House Party,* the best "rap movie" yet made. Good writers and rappers, they're also *great* dancers . . . and Kid's eight-inch fade wins his crew much respect in a world in which the pursuit of the perfect haircut is nearly as important as the search for the perfect beat.

Says Play: "We believe in leading by example, rather than preaching. We went to school, we plan on continuing school later on, and we don't do drugs. The rewards we've gotten from following that path are greater than those of the negative forces . . . and we don't have to worry about somebody knocking on the door one morning to take it all away."

From "Rollin' With Kid 'n' Play"

**Now we're the stars of stage, wax, and
    video
We're here to tear it up, so come on, here
    we go
Pump it up, this is high-powered stuff
Kid 'n' Play can't get enough
Of that funky go-go-go rhythm
You wanted a dope jam, well, that's what
    we're givin'
We're headed for fame 'cause Kid 'n' Play's
    driven
Boy, we don't care, and large is how we're
    livin'
'Cause we stay paid
You know the boys have got it made
See, I'm the Tramp
And I'm the fella with the high-top fade
Gettin' down to the sound,
You know we're 'bout to turn it out
Roll with Kid 'n' Play, everybody shout!**

Manhattan, 1987.

53

Left: **Play 'n' Kid. Manhattan, 1988.**

Salt, Spinderella, and Pepa. Manhattan, 1988.

salt 'n' pepa

Salt 'n' Pepa were the first female rappers to decline to play by the restrictive rules set up for women in rap. Before them, female rappers tended to address themselves to the men in the house, either as Fly Girls or Nagging Wives. The attitude toward other women—strict keep-your-hands-off-my-man hostility—was similarly one-dimensional.

But, as the title of their very first album, *Hot, Cool, and Vicious* (1986), suggests, Salt 'n' Pepa started out with a whole arsenal of moods and moves, all of which they've continued to deploy in what is still essentially a man's world. This intellectual and emotional range, in combination with the decidedly pop sensibility that grows out of their conviction that "rap is for everyone," won the trio the first platinum album ever awarded to female rappers . . . and the second, as well. Nominated in 1989 for the first Grammy ever bestowed on rappers, Salt 'n' Pepa decided to boycott the awards ceremony because the presentation of that award would not be televised. It was yet another demonstration of their independence and integrity . . . and of their pride in rap.

The trio from Queens, New York, consists of Cheryl James (Salt), Sandy Denton (Pepa), and Dee Dee Roper (Spinderella, their deejay). Notes Salt: "Girls usually depend on guys for everything. We're not like that. We're like three sisters. We think a lot alike on most things and we keep each other sane."

55

At the Idolmakers studio, Queens, 1989.

Manhattan, 1987.

eric b. & rakim

Eric B. & Rakim exploded onto the scene in the summer of 1986 with "Eric B. Is President" on tiny Harlem-based Zakia Records. Musically, deejay/producer Eric Barrier (of East Elmhurst, Queens) was pioneering the sampling of beats from the records of James Brown, a move that re-emphasized the primacy of funk in rap. Vocally, the rapper Rakim (William Griffin of Wyandanch, Long Island)—with his ultra-smooth and insinuating style—was pioneering a clear-cut alternative to the chest beating established by the Run-DMC/LL Cool J school of rap. Imagewise, they came off like a mutant hybrid of Al Capone, Barry White, and a Muslim penitent, combining gangster attitude with an absolutely unashamed brand of commodity fetishism and (in Rakim's case) an unquestionably sincere strain of religious devotion. They proceeded to hit through the end of the decade with "I Know You Got Soul," "I Ain't No Joke," "Paid in Full," "Follow the Leader," "Microphone Fiend," and into the Nineties with "Let the Rhythm Hit 'Em."

Rakim, in 1988, on how he writes: "I go downstairs where my equipment is, I sit down, turn all the lights off, and listen to some jazz or somethin' like that. Then I listen to the track I'm gonna write off of. Then I got this one spotlight that I put on the paper, so that's where I concentrate. Ain't nothin' else goin' on but the paper.

"I want to tell people about mistakes they could make before they happen. You've got to give the crowd something that will benefit them, and not just get onstage and talk about yourself all the time."

From "Mahogany"

Me and Eric B. was coolin' at the Palladium
Seen a all-world cover-girl, I said, "Hey, lady, I'm . . .
Sorry if you're in a rush, don't let me hold you up
Or intervene or interrupt
But you got the look. I wanna get to know you better."
I had to let her know, but, yo, I didn't sweat her
'Cause if you woulda seen what I was seein'
Almost looked Korean, but European
When she spoke, her accent was self-explanatory
Even her body language told a story
Her name was Mahogany, twin's name was Ebony
I said, "My name is Ra and this is Eric B."
Since the music was loud, I said, "Let's take a walk."
So we could talk and see New York
Showtime didn't start until one o'clock
"But once I entered your mind, I wouldn't want to stop
Caress your thoughts 'til we was thinkin' the same
Calm your nerves, massage your brain
Each moment's a mineral, poetry protein
Verse is a vitamin, effect's like codeine
Then tell me how ya feel when I reveal the pill
That'll heal your pain 'cause I'm real."
She musta o'd'ed 'cause she couldn't re-sist
She spoke slowly when she told me this
She said, "Over me, you're going crazy."
She rubbed me on my chest and called me Mr. Sexy

She said she want my kids and help me make my next g
Tell me I ain't finesse Mahogany

. . . It's funny how time flies when you're havin' fun
We got close and it was almost one
She kissed me slow but you know how far a kiss can go:
Fuck around and miss the show
So I told her to hold that thought real tight
We could finish where we left off later on tonight
Back to the scene of the crime on time
As they introduced the fiend of a rhyme
She stood in the crowd with a bird's eye view of me
Thinkin' of later on what she could do to me
From the back of the room I could see her eyes gloom
Patient, but hopin' that the show was over soon
As the place was ripped in half, she made her way to the front row
So I said, "Let's go."
I packed my mike as they screamed for a encore
The speakers were blown, plus my mike was sore
But, sorry, I got places to go, ladies to see

57

And she could tell me how crazy she was
  over me
We drove off, she said she liked the way
  that I performed
And couldn't wait to get soft and warm
I said, "I was watchin' you watchin' me.
Looks I received made it hard to emcee."
I could take a hint so I knew that she
Wanted my agony agony agony in her
  body
Showed her some sights, then I took her
  to the condo
She was pipin' hot, but I kept my calm so

She axed how come I don't smile. I said,
  "Everything's fine
But I'm in a New York state of mind."
As we reached the kingdom
She said, bring some
Champagne, she'll entertain, then sing
  some
Sentimental songs real gentle
It hit the spot and you know where it
  went to
As we embraced, I felt her heart pumpin'
I knew she was in the mood for somethin'
So I laid on my back and relaxed

It wasn't the Perignon that made her col-
  lapse
Over me, she was goin' crazy
She rubbed me on the chest and called
  me Mr. Sexy
She said she want my kids and help me
  make my next g
Tell me I ain't finesse Mahogany

58

Manhattan, 1987.

heavy d & the boyz

Heavy D is rap's update of Jackie Gleason, the fat man America loves to love. Born Dwight Myers in Jamaica and raised in "money-earnin' Mount Vernon," New York, Heavy is big (six-foot-four, 260 pounds), but he's no joke. Indeed, he's graceful and dignified, a combination that enables him to declare with much credibility, "Girls, they girls, they love me, the overweight lover Heavy D." Arsenio Hall claims he was inspired to create his cartoonish Chunky A rap alter ego after watching Heavy slay the young ladies in performance.

Working with producer Teddy Riley and manager Andre Harrell, Heavy pioneered "new jack swing" from the rap side of the rap–R & B equation in songs of his own, and as a guest artist on LeVert's "Just Coolin'." His overall strategy: "We're trying to have a straightforward, clean-cut image, but cool at the same time."

Manhattan, 1990.

59

With Scott LaRock, standing. The Bronx, 1987.

boogie down productions

From "You Must Learn"

It's calm yet wild, the style that I speak
Deal with facts and you'll never get weak
  in the heart
In fact, you'll start to illuminate
Knowledge to others in a song. Let me
  demonstrate
The force of knowledge. Knowledge
  reigns supreme
The ignorant are ripped to smithereens
What do you mean when you say I'm re-
  bellious
'Cause I don't accept everything that
  you're tellin' us?
What are you sellin' us? The Creator dwells
  in us
I sit in your unknown class while you're
  failing us
I failed your class 'cause I ain't wit' your
  reasoning
You try to make me you by seasoning
Up my mind with "See Jane run.
See John walk" in a hard-core New York
Come on now. It's like a chocolate cow:
It doesn't exist, no way, no how
It seems to me that in a school that's
  ebony
African history should be pumped up
  steadily
But it's not, and this has got to stop:
"See Spot run. Run get Spot."
Insulting to a black mentality
A black way of life or a jet-black family
So I include with one concern:
That you must learn!

Boogie Down Productions' original mission was to restore some hip-hop respectability to the Bronx. By 1986, when BDP started making their first singles, Queens, in the forms of Run-DMC, LL Cool J, and Eric B & Rakim, had long since become the creative center of the music. Then BDP (named in homage to "the boogie-down Bronx") hit with "The Bridge Is Over" and "South Bronx" and all of a sudden the Bronx was no longer a has-been.

The group consisted of deejay Scott LaRock (born Scott Sterling) and KRS-ONE (an acronym for Knowledge Reigns Supreme Over Nearly Everyone, born plain old Lawrence Parker). They'd met at a men's shelter in the Bronx, where LaRock, a college grad, was a counselor and the homeless Kris a client. Together they released "Criminal Minded" on B-Boy Records, hailed by Harry Allen in the *Village Voice* as "the most unrelenting audio document of black urban motion, paranoia, good humor, and brotherhood this decade." Not long afterward, on August 27, 1987, Scott was shot dead in the Bronx, trying to intercede on behalf of a friend in an argument. He was twenty-five years old.

Kris has gone on alone to establish himself as "the Teacher," one of the most respected figures in hip-hop. He was the central creative force on the Stop the Violence Movement's "Self-Destruction" (1988), an all-star benefit record and video (featuring Public Enemy, Kool Moe Dee, Stetsasonic, MC Lyte, and others) that condemned black-on-black violence, one of the great scourges of America's black communities today. By the fall of 1989 he was writing op-ed pieces for *The New York Times* on the shortcomings due to racism of the city's schools' curricula. By the spring of 1990 he had lectured by invitation at Columbia and Harvard universities.

He has said: "I speak to the human intelligence. I want to show kids another way to deal with things. We can deal with things by being intelligent and dealing with our problems head on." And: "I don't follow what rap is doing because my private opinion is that I *am* rap, and wherever I go, rap goes."

61

Manhattan, 1988.

62 *Left to right:* **Flavor Flav, Chuck D, and Terminator X. Manhattan, 1987.**

public enemy

From "Fight the Power"

Elvis was a hero to most
But he never meant shit to me, you see
Straight-out racist, that sucker was
Simple and plain
Motherfuck him *and* John Wayne
'Cause I'm black and I'm proud
I'm ready and hyped, plus I'm amped
Most of my heroes don't appear on no
     stamps
Sample a look back, you look and find
Nothing but rednecks for four hundred
     years, if you check
"Don't Worry, Be Happy" was a number
     one jam
Damn! If *I* say it, you can slap me right
     here
Get it!

Let's get this party started right
Right on!
C'mon!
What we got to say:
Power to the people, no delay!
Make everybody see
In order to fight the powers that be

Carlton Ridenhour/Keith Shocklee (James Henry Boxley)/
Eric Sadler. Copyright © 1989 by Your Mothers Music/Def
American Songs Inc.

Public Enemy has turned out to be the most aptly named group in the history of rap. They emerged out of Hempstead, Long Island, and Adelphi University in 1987 and immediately established brand-new highwater marks for both high-energy beats and inspirational rhymes. In the process, they vastly enlarged the intellectual scope of the music and its audience. Suddenly, rap wasn't just for kids; older rockers, black and white alike, now found themselves compelled to tune in. Indeed, Public Enemy may have singlehandedly accomplished one of their original objectives: to turn rap away from what they called the "cold gettin' dumb" movement and in the direction of something a little more nourishing. As group leader Chuck D (Carlton Ridenhour) put it: "It's about gold *brains* now, not gold chains."

Unfortunately, there was considerable internal disagreement about what made up the rest of the group's agenda. These conflicts surfaced when the group's "Minister of Information," Professor Griff (Richard Griffin), gave an anti-Semitic interview to writer David Mills of the *Washington Times* in May 1989. Caught (or so he thought) between the Jewish community and the black community, Chuck D backpedaled, bobbed and weaved, and then disbanded the group. Just in time, too. Spike Lee's *Do the Right Thing*—featuring Public Enemy's "Fight the Power" on the soundtrack—was just about to be released, and the Jewish Defense Organization was threatening to organize a nationwide boycott.

But the crew was back touring before the summer was out, with Griff still in the lineup, and the controversy erupted anew. Chuck, who has a genius for dousing a fire with gasoline, devoted his next single to the mess. Entitled "Welcome to the Terrordome" and released in January 1990, it ignited charges that Chuck himself was anti-Semitic.

Griff finally left the group on his own in March 1990 and released an album under his own name (Professor Griff and the Last Asiatic Disciples) on the Luke Skyywalker label at about the same time that Public Enemy released their third album, "Fear of a Black Planet."

The crux of their extramusical problems may be that Public Enemy Number One, Chuck D, is not a thinker/orator/leader on a par with Malcolm X. It is a testament to his greatness as a musician/poet/sloganeer, however, that one even wishes he were. (And thank God for Flavor Flav, Public Enemy's self-described "friendly ghost" and saving grace. He ain't no joke.)

Professor Griff. Manhattan, 1988.

63

64

With Master T, Big Drew, and K. Rock. Brooklyn, 1990.

mc lyte

From "I Cram to Understand U (Sam)"

I used to be in love with this guy named
Sam
I don't know why 'cause he had a head
like that of a clam
But you couldn't tell me nothin' 'cause
Sam was number one
'Cause to me, oh, my gosh, he was one in
a million
I shoulda knew the consequences right
from the start
That he'd use me for my money and then
break my heart
But like a fool in love, I fell for his game
But I got mines, so I show no shame

. . . My cousin said she saw you with this
lady named Miss C.
Well I'm clawing on my thoughts, I wonder
who she could be
You're spendin' all your time with her and
not a second with me
They said you spend your money on her
and you're with her night and day
Her name starts with a *c* and it ends with
a *k*
I strain my brains lookin' for a name to fit
this spelling
But I just couldn't do it 'cause my heart
kept yelling
Burning, beggin' for affection from you,
Sam
But just like a test, I cram to understand
you

Just like a test
Just just like a test
Just just like a test
I cram to understand you

Then there came a time you started
lookin' kinda thin
Asked you why, you said, "Exercise. Tryin'
to stay slim."
I bought it even though I knew it was a lie
'Cause it really didn't matter, you were
still lookin' fly
But, oh no, oh no, you started askin' me
for money
Butter me up, beg me, and call me your
honey
So I gave you two yards and then I gave
you one more
You picked up your jacket and you flew
out the door
You came back an hour later and you
asked for a ten
I said, "I only have a twenty." You said,
"Give me that then."
I said, "Nope, I tell ya now, you better
stop slobbin'.
Find you a job or you better start rob-
bin'."

. . . But now I see you at Empire every
Sunday
Juicin' the girls up for some money and a
lay
But every time I see you doin' it, I just
ruin it
Tell how ya on crack, smoke, sniff, and
chewin' it
As for this girl, Miss C, oh well, I was
Shocked as hell when I heard, Samuel
When your homeboys told me, I almost
went wack
That the girl you was addicted to, her
name was crack

Just like a test
Just just like a test
Just just like a test
I cram to understand you

MC Lyte, born Lana Moorer in Queens and raised in Brooklyn, began rapping at the age of twelve. She debuted with a big splash in 1988 with "I Cram to Understand U (Sam)," and helped to bridge the rap-rock gap by contributing a guest vocal to Sinead O'Connor's "I Want Your (Hands on Me)."

In March 1990 she said: "I'm nineteen years old and I've been rapping professionally for about three and a half years now. A couple of guys in school used to rap, and I started rapping with them. We did it for fun, no instruments, just banging on our desks. At first, they wrote raps for me, but eventually I started writing myself.

"Now I write all my own raps, wherever, whenever. Sometimes all the rhymes come in spurts. Whatever I feel like saying on record, I say on record. From the beginning, with 'I Cram to Understand U,' I mostly rhyme about not being taken advantage of, not being a pushover.

"After this rap stuff, I hope to go into management . . . not just musicians, but actresses and actors, too."

Parrish and Erick. Babylon, Long Island, 1989.

epmd

From "You Gots to Chill"

Relax your mind
Let your conscience be free
And get down to the sounds of EPMD
While you should keep quiet while the
    emcee rap
But if you're tired, then go take a nap
Or stay awake and watch the show I take
Because right now I'm 'bout to shake and
    bake
The E-r-i-c-k is my name I spell
Thanks to the clientele, yo, I rock well
I'm not an emcee who's talkin' all that
    junk
About who can beat who. Sound like a
    punk
I just get down and I go for mine
Say, "Check, one, two" and run down the
    line

To the average emcee I'm known as the
    Terminator
Funky beat maker, new-jack exterminator
To destroy and unemploy when your
    rhymes are nonvoid
Never sweatin' your girl
(Why, P?)
'Cause she's a skeezoid
When I'm on the scene I always rock the
    spot
I grab the steel with the crown on the top
In the beginning
I like to let my rhymes flow
And at twelve I press cruise control
Sit back and relax
Grab my bozack
Maintain emcee's while the Double-E max
Always calm under pressure
No need to act ill
Listen when I tell you, boy
You gots to chill

EPMD crashed onto the scene during the summer of 1988 with "You Gots to Chill" and *Strictly Business* . . . and proceeded to wreck the black sales charts, effortlessly shouldering aside rap records by Public Enemy, Jazzy Jeff & the Fresh Prince, Rob Base, and Run-DMC, as well as smash *pop* records by George .Michael, Michael Jackson, Prince, and Sade.

They're low tech and low tempo, their subject is almost invariably their own deffness as rappers, and (in Erick's case, at least) they're mush-mouthed in an idiom where the elocutionary dexterity of a Shakespearian actor is damn near standard equipment. They're also deeply funky and very street. A two-man crew from Brentwood, Long Island, composed of Erick Sermon and Parrish Smith, their name is an acronym for Erick and Parrish Making Dollars. And along with making dancers and lovers of rhyme very happy, that is precisely what they do.

Says Parrish: "Erick writes his lyrics and I write my lyrics. If I don't feel his are tough enough, I let him know, and vice versa. If we agree on it, we use it. If not, we don't. Make it or break it."

With posse. West Babylon, Long Island, 1988.

2 live crew

Virtually every year since, say, 1986, one rap act or another has been a target for the malign attention·of one special interest group or another that otherwise demonstrates absolutely no interest in rap or, for that matter, in black youth. In '86 it was Run-DMC. In '87 the Beastie Boys edged out LL Cool J for top honors. In '88 it was Public Enemy. In '89 Public Enemy and NWA finished in a dead heat, with NWA under fire from the FBI and Public Enemy under fire from the combined forces of the Jewish Defense Organization, the Anti-Defamation League, the Simon Weisenthal Center for Holocaust Studies, and the Parents Music Resource Center. Halfway through 1990 the 2 Live Crew was ahead of the rest of the pack by about twenty lengths.

It seems that the law enforcement community in the Miami area (the Crew's home base), prodded by local right-wing religious zealots, doesn't like the 2 Live Crew. Their records are too dirty, they say. They encourage the abuse of women, they say. There oughta be a law, they say. And so, the governor of the state called for an investigation. The federal judge down there declared the album *As Nasty as They Want to Be* obscene. The sheriff of Broward County arrested two of the members of the group following an adults-only show, and then began to arrest the owners of local record stores who continued to sell the album despite the court's ruling.

In fact, whether or not the record is "obscene" (a decision that will likely be reviewed by the Supreme Court), it is clearly misogynistic, and the makers of this book condemn that misogyny. Still, we don't agree that the entire weight of the state should be dropped on the Crew's shoulders. In fact, we don't think the state should be involved at all. We do believe the 2 Live Crew are being singled out for political reasons.

Figure it out for yourself. Are the 2 Live Crew the only source of misogyny in the Florida area? No. Have there been any other books, movies, records declared obscene and banned in Broward County? No. Have any of the kingpins of Miami's porn industry, one of the largest in the country, been arrested lately for violations of local community standards? No.

Wonder what the hell is going on? It's been referred to as the Politics of Distraction. American conservatives would rather do anything than address the real-life social conditions that create the artistic expressions they so deplore. Columnist Gary Stein of the Ft. Lauderdale *Sun-Sentinel* X-rayed the situation with regard to Florida Governor Bob Martinez, who began calling for a statewide criminal investigation of the 2 Live Crew in February 1990, just about the time that some polls showed that he might "have trouble winning re-election against anybody but Charles Manson."

"If Martinez has the time and the inclination to go after rap music, that says to me that he has the rest of the state's problems solved," rapped Stein. "Crime, you say? What crime problem in Florida? Our governor has it licked. . . . Drugs? Did someone mention crack cocaine? Not a problem anymore. Not in Florida. . . . Education? Education is no longer a problem. The dropout rate is no longer a problem. Our education system in Florida is the very best in the country. . . . The homeless? Are you crazy? There is no longer a problem with the homeless."

Funny, right? But not if you're Luther Campbell and the 2 Live Crew. Don't let the lunatics in *your* community get away with this kind of thing.

Manhattan, 1990.

69

From "Me So Horny" (Clean Version)

Sittin' at home watchin' Arsenio Hall

So I got my black book for a freak to
call

Picked up the telephone and dialed
the seven digits

Said, "Yo! This is Marquis, baby, are
you down with it?"

I arrived at her house, knocked on the
door

Not havin' no idea of what the night
had in store

I'm like a dog in heat, a freak without
warning

I have an appetite for love, 'cause me
so horny

Girls always ask me why I'm up so
much

I say, "What's wrong, baby doll, with
bein' a nut?"

But my nature is risin' and you
shouldn't be mad

I won't tell your momma, if you don't
tell your dad

I know he'll be disgusted when he sees
your clothes all messed up

Won't your momma be so mad if she
knew you'd just been had

But I'm a freak in heat, a dog without
warning

My appetite is love 'cause me so horny

From "Me So Horny" (Nasty Version)

Sittin' at home with my dick all hard

So I got the black book for a freak to
call

Picked up the telephone, then dialed
the seven digits

Said, "Yo! This is Marquis, baby. Are
you down with it?"

I arrived at her house, knocked on the
door

Not havin' no idea of what the night
had in store

I'm like a dog in heat, a freak without
warning

I have an appetite for sex, 'cause me
so horny

Girls always ask me why I fuck so much

I just say, "What's wrong, baby doll,
with a quick nut?"

'Cause you're the one and you
shouldn't be mad

I won't tell your momma, if you don't
tell your dad

I know he'll be disgusted when he sees
your pussy busted

Won't your momma be so mad if she
knew I got that ass?

I'm a freak in heat, a dog without
warning

My appetite is sex 'cause me so horny

From "Banned in the USA"

The First Amendment gave us freedom
of speech

So watcha sayin'? It didn't include me?

I like to party and have a good time

There's nothin' but pleasure written in
our rhymes

I know you don't think we'll ever quit

We got some people on our side who
won't take your lip

We're gonna do all the things we
wanna do

You can't stand to see a brother get as
rich as you

This is the Nineties and we're comin'
on strong

Sayin' things and doin' things that
you're sayin's wrong

Wisen up 'cause on Election Day

We'll see who's banned in the USA

70

Manhattan, 1990.

rob base and dj e-z rock

From "It Takes Two"

I wanna rock right now
I'm Rob Base and I came to get down
I'm not internationally known
But I'm known to rock the microphone
Because I get stupid, I mean outrageous
Stay away from me if you're contagious
'Cause I'm a winner, no, not a loser
To be an emcee is what I choose-uh
Ladies love me, girls adore me
I mean even the ones who never saw me
   like
The way that I rhyme at a show
The reason why? Man, I don't know
So let's go 'cause . . .

It takes two to make a thing go right
It takes two to make it outta sight

Copyright © Protoons Inc./Hikim Music/ASCAP

Rob Base and dj E-Z Rock won their immortality on the strength of "It Takes Two." Built on James Brown's 1972 production of Lyn Collins's "Think (About It)," theirs is not only one of the greatest rap records in history, it was declared "the number one single *of all time*" by Frank Owen in *Spin.* The ultra-catchy rap/singing hybrid ruled the airwaves and the streets throughout the summer and into the fall of 1988. It was followed by another rap/singing hybrid called "Joy and Pain," which was damn near as irresistible as "It Takes Two."

Base (Robert Ginyard) and Rock (Rodney Bryce) grew up together in Harlem. Says Base: "I always wanted to rap. I had my mind set since I was fifteen. There was never anything else I wanted to do. My parents were behind me, but scared for me.

" 'It Takes Two' was done on the spur of the moment. I didn't know what I was going to do when I went in and did that—it just came out that way.

"They're saying that I got lucky on the first one, but I told 'em: 'Well, the new one [*The Incredible Base*] is almost gold already. Must be lucky on this one, too!' "

Left: **Manhattan, 1988.**

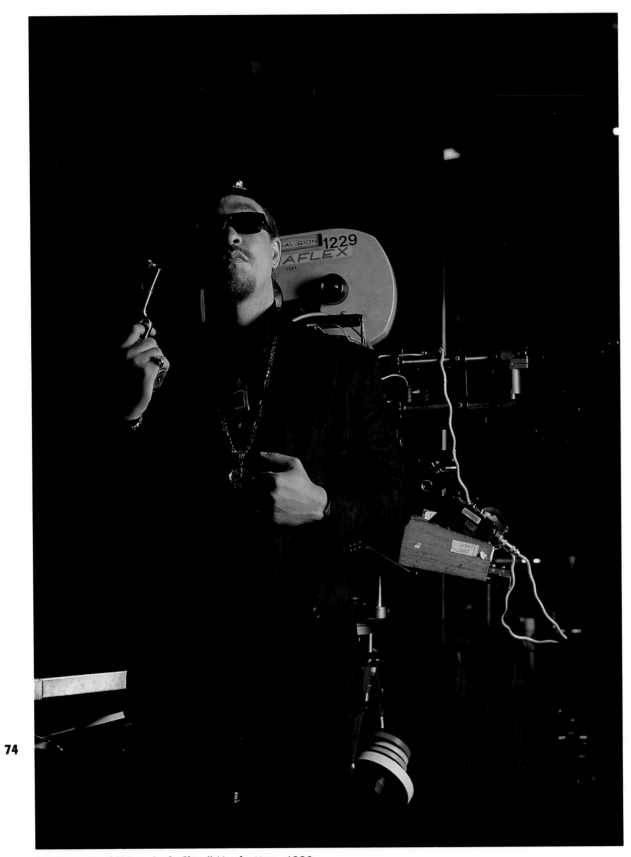

On the set of "New Jack City." Manhattan, 1990.

ice-t

Ice-T was the first rapper from Los Angeles to get respect in New York. He took his name from Iceberg Slim, author of a series of enormously popular ghetto novels, and called his first album *Rhyme Pays* (1987). But it wasn't until he performed the title song in *Colors*, a movie about the L.A. gang scene released the next year, that he really began to make a national name for himself. Since then Ice has developed as a passionate and articulate spokesman for rap (he's testified in Congress on the subject of gangs and drugs), as a businessman (his production company is called the Rhyme Syndicate), and as an actor. Janette shot this photo on the set of *New Jack City*, a movie in which Ice plays an undercover narcotics cop.

The World According to Ice-T: "Freedom is a great concept, but it's not generally available. They tell you to say what's on your mind, but they don't really want to hear. There's limits on what you can do, if you want to keep your job. You never know who you're going to offend or when the PMRC is gonna come knocking on your door."

From "Freedom of Speech"

"You have the right to remain silent . . ."

Fuck that right!
I want the right to talk
I want the right to speak
I want the right to walk
Where I wanna, yell and I'm gonna
Tell and rebel every time I'm on a
Microphone, on a stage, cold illin'
The knowledge I drop will be heard by
  millions
We ain't the problems, we ain't the villains
It's the suckers deprivin' the truth from
  our children
You can't hide the fact, Jack
There's violence in the streets every day
Any fool can recognize that
But you try to lie and lie
And say America's some motherfuckin'
  apple pie
Yo! You gotta be high to believe
That you gonna change the world by a
  sticker on a record sleeve
'Cause once you take away my right to
  speak
Everybody in the world's up shit creek

Freedom of speech!
Yeahhhh . . . Just watch what you say
Freedom of speech!
Yeahhhh . . . You better watch what you
  say
Freedom of speech!
Just watch what you say

Freedom of speech!
Let 'em take it from me
Then they'll take it from you
Then what you gonna do?

Let 'em censor books?
Let 'em censor art?
PMRC, this is where the witchhunt
  starts
You'll censor what we see, we read,
  we hear, we learn
—The books will burn
You better think it out
We should be able to say anything
Our lungs were meant to shout
Say what we feel, yell out what's real
Even though it may not bring mass
  appeal
Your opinion is yours, my opinion is
  mine
If you don't like what I'm sayin', fine
But don't close it—always keep an
  open mind
A man who fails to listen is blind
We only got one right left in the
  world today
Let me have it—or throw the Consti-
  tution away.

big daddy kane

As I walk the streets of Hollywood Boulevard

Thinkin' how hard it was to those that starred

In the movies, portrayin' the roles

Of butlers and maids, slaves and ho's

Many intelligent black men seemed

To look uncivilized when on the screen

Like I guess I figured you to play some jigaboo

On the plantation. What else can a nigger do?

And black women in this profession:

As for playing a lawyer, out of the question

For what they play "Aunt Jemima" is the perfect term

Even if now she got a perm

So let's make our own movies like Spike Lee

'Cause the roles being offered don't strike me

There's nothing that the black man could use to earn

Burn, Hollywood, burn!

Big Daddy Kane is not easy. He is pimp and preacher, a writer and a dancer. Among the angriest and most street of rappers, he was invited in the fall of 1989 to rhyme alongside notorious firebrands Chuck D and Ice Cube on Public Enemy's "Burn Hollywood Burn." At just about the same moment, he was becoming widely recognized as one of the most striking-*looking* black achievers since Grace Jones.

Kane was just twenty years old when he hit for the first time as a solo artist (with "Ain't No Half-Steppin" in the summer of 1988), but he'd already established himself—via hits for Roxanne Shante and Biz Markie—as a veteran writer and producer. A native of Brooklyn's Bedford-Stuyvesant neighborhood and a present-day resident of Queens, Kane is a serious student of soul, prone to drive around town studying, say, a tape of a live concert by Dee Clark, a concert recorded several years before Kane's birth.

During the winter of 1988–89 Kane hit the road with Ice-T in a speaking tour of black high schools in Detroit, New York, Atlanta, Washington, Chicago, St. Louis, and Milwaukee. The tour delivered an antidrug message to the kids from a couple of artists they respected. "Words can change a person, change the world," Kane explained. "I try to tell the kids about the importance of education and the power of words."

77

Left: **Manhattan, 1988.**

Right: **Manhattan, 1988**

78

Ed Lover, T-Money, and Doctor Dre. Manhattan, 1989.

doctor dre and ed lover

From "Pump That Bass" by Original Concept

Get a little stupid
Get a little stupid
Get get a little stupid
And pump that bass!

From "The Famous Mr. Ed" by Ed Lover

For years I've been at it
Just like a fanatic
I'll dust my funky rhymes off
That I kept up in the attic

Doctor Dre and Ed Lover, the congenial b-boy hosts of the daily edition of "Yo! MTV Raps," had never met before they started working together on the show. Dre was an old friend of the show's original executive producer, Peter Dougherty, who knew Dre back when the big guy was touring as the Beastie Boys' deejay. (He'd also gained some notoriety as a rap radio jock, and as the leader of Def Jam Recordings act Original Concept, perpetrators of the deathless "Pump That Bass.") Ed was your basic class clown, a lifelong musician, and a childhood friend of the show's original producer, Ted Demme. After the weekend version of "Yo!," hosted by Fab 5 Freddy, blasted off, each bigwig nominated his own guy to host the planned daily version. There was supposed to be only one host, but Ed and Dre hit it off so well that the producers made room for the two of them. The rest is history.

As for the future, who knows? Network TV? Movies? A line of sportswear? A trademark cologne? And finally, at the end of their distinguished career, positions in the cabinet of President Young MC, by which time we'll surely be calling it the Black House.

Original Concept (with the Rapper G, right). Manhattan, 1988.

80

Left to right: **Mase, Trugoy, and Posdnuous. West Babylon, Long Island, 1990.**

de la soul

From "Me, Myself, and I"

Mirror, mirror on the wall
Tell me, mirror, what is wrong
Can it be my De La clothes?
Or is it just my De La Soul?
What I do ain't make-believe
People say I sit and try
But when it comes to being De La
It's just me, myself, and I
Now you tease my Plug One style?
And my Plug One spectacles?
You say Plug One and Two are hippies
No, we're not, that's pure plug bull
Always pushing that we formed an image
There's no need to lie
When it comes to being Plug One
It's just me, myself, and I

Proud, I'm proud of what I am
Poems I speak, the Plug Two type
Please, oh please, let Plug Two be
Himself, not what you read or write
Write is wrong when hype is written
On the Soul (De La, that is)
Style is surely our own thing
Not the false disguise of show biz
De La Soul is from the soul
And this fact I can't deny
Strictly from the Dan called Stuckey
And from me, myself, and I.

De La Soul was something brand-new in rap. For all of their relatedness to the other players on the set when they emerged in the fall of 1988, De La Soul might just as well have been (as one of their later compositions would put it) "transmitting live from Mars." Essentially, they set themselves up from the beginning as the anti-b-boys of hip-hop. They wore no gold chains, didn't pound their chests and brag about themselves, rapped dreamily about the D.A.I.S.Y. Age (Da Inner Sound, Y'all), and laughed a lot.

They came from Amityville, Long Island, and like Run-DMC, were comprised of two emcees (Posdnuos and Trugoy the Dove) and a deejay (Pace Master Mase)—although they didn't even accept those antique terms of description. "Is being the best m.c.'s a main drive for Pos and Dove?" they asked rhetorically in their self-written record company bio. "Of course not. We are public speakers, not m.c.'s. Is being the best d.j. a main drive for Mase? Of course not. He's a p.a. system, not a d.j." Oblique where Run was direct, De La Soul couldn't even write a "sucker emcees" rant without reimagining it as someone digging "potholes in my lawn."

Their obvious intelligence, their nerd pride, their baggy clothes, psychedelic colors, off-kilter haircuts, and—of course—their superdef beats and rhymes made De La Soul an immediate smash with younger black kids, slightly older black college kids and their white friends, and virtually every music critic in the world. Their first album, "3 Feet High and Rising," sold over a million copies. Their second was due out by the end of 1990.

the jungle brothers

From "Tribe Vibes"

I heard the bongos
Bongo beats from the jungle
A ritual a ritual a ritual a ritual
Fire in the middle, I chant a little riddle
I saw a man on the side takin' pictures
But some of us never paid him no mind
Click click! Flash flash! Boom bash!
Smashed up his camera, weakened his
    stamina
We didn't kill 'im, we painted him black
Put him down wit' the tribe, put 'im down
    wit' the pack
Took his gun and took his rifle
Changed his clothes and told 'im to sit
    still
He tried to run but there was nowhere to
    hide
So at the end he gave in 'cause he felt
    the tribe vibes

The Jungle Brothers may have released *Done by the Forces of Nature* (November 1989) several months before Public Enemy's *Fear of a Black Planet*, but the former feels like it takes up where the latter leaves off. On *Fear* Public Enemy is, as ever, waist deep in the muck, still fighting the power, still hacking away at the tentacles of white cultural imperialism even as they dream of the Eden of a black planet. *Forces of Nature,* by contrast, is a long, seductive letter from the Garden by a group of pioneers who've already taken up residence there.

The world of the JBs is Afrocentric, communalistic, antimaterialistic, peaceful, productive, sensual, *and* intellectual. If this were the Sixties, they'd be described as cultural revolutionaries, as opposed to political revolutionaries. That is, the Jungle Brothers give the impression of *living* the revolution around the clock (and creating more revolution by example), and apparently don't feel the need or usefulness of storming the barricades. In short, there is something magical about them. (And they sure can write.)

The crew is comprised of Afrika Baby Bambaataa (Nathaniel Hall), Mike G (Michael Small), and deejay Sammy B (Sammy Burwell). Afrika is from Brooklyn, Mike and Sammy from Harlem, but all three trace their heritage back to the beginning of hip-hop in the persons of Afrika Bambaataa (their mentor) and DJ Red Alert (their former manager).

Says Bam of his children: "The Jungle Brothers are very well-schooled in all of the music of the planet, very innovative and very respectful. They're the Sly & the Family Stone of hip-hop, taking the music in a new direction. And now *they're* influencing *me.*"

83

Left. Bottom row, *left to right:* **Afrika Baby Bombaataa, Mike G, and Sammy B. Manhattan, 1990.**

84

Los Angeles, 1990.

the boo-yaa t.r.i.b.e.

From "6 Bad Brothers"

Poem-Throwin' Samoan on the microphone
You like the sound, don't touch the bass
  tone
Drop it, you can't stop it
You wish you would, kick it in the 'hood
You never could, good
Better than bad, the new fad
But your Six-Four could never touch my
  Cad
The Granddad, now you call me superior
You know my name, but me, I never hear
  of ya

. . . Bad motherfuckers, six wanted hus-
  tlers
Down for the count, we'll kill you with a
  muffler
Silence! Ssssh! they say real bad boys
  move in silence
But the hard loud ones are more violent

. . . You got it like this, We got it like
  that
Man, you ain't be got no gat
Boo-Yaa Tribe is the winning team
Why you say that?
We get the loudest screams!

By P. Devoux, D. Devoux, S. Silva, and Joe Nicolo. Copyright © 1990 by Ackee Music Inc., Boo-Yaa T.R.I.B.E. Music.

The Boo-Yaa T.R.I.B.E. consists of members of a Los Angeles–based family of Samoan background named Devoux. As youths they ran with a large and notorious local gang called the Bloods, but decided to channel their energies into music following the murder of one of their brothers in the drug war. Their first album, *New Funky Nation,* was released in 1990.

Says Ted "the Godfather" Devoux: "We grew up poor—we were evicted from three houses—but it's not true that the only way for kids to make money is by getting involved with drugs. We live in the land of opportunity, and what counts is the person, not the environment. My mother thought my brother needed a new environment after he got involved with gangs, so she sent him to Hawaii, but he just started a gang there. When he got killed, I had to do something to get my brothers on a new track. That's why we do these things as a family, because when you're a family, you can watch out for each other.

"The thing about Samoan families, it's not just a handful of people, 'cause my dad has six brothers, two sisters. Within that six brothers, the least sons they have is three. In my family I have eight brothers. My dad's brother, Larry, he's got six boys and one girl. My auntie, she has three boys, and my other uncle, he has five boys and one girl. That's why we're so close-knit: you mess with one, you mess with all of us. You're talking about an army."

Says Paul "Riddler" Devoux: "In our days when we were gangbanging, 'boo-yaa!' was the sound of a shotgun. [Now] that's the feedback when we go to a club: like *'boo-yaa!'* Everyone looks at us like we killed someone. But it's just us, just coming down to enjoy ourselves."

With their sumo-wrestling brother. Los Angeles, 1990.

85

86

Manhattan, 1990.

a tribe called quest

From "Can I Kick It?"

To all the people who can quest like a
   tribe does
Before this did you really know what live
   was?
Comprehend to the track for it's wide, cuz
Getting mentions on the tip of the vibe
   buzz
Rock 'n' roll to the beat of the funk fuzz
Wipe your feet really good on the rhythm
   rug
If you feel the urge to freak, do the jitter-
   bug
Come and spread your arms if you really
   need a hug
Afrocentric living gives a big shrug
A life filled with fun: that's what we love
A lower plateau is what we're above
If you dis us, we won't even think of
Will Nipper the doggie give a big shove?
This rhythm really fits like a snug glove
Like a box of positives, it's a plus love
As the Tribe flies high like a dove

A Tribe Called Quest builds their outlook right into the name of their New York-based crew, which consists of Q-Tip, Phife, Ali, and Jarobi. Like the other members of the Native Tongues Posse, Quest is distinguished by their easygoing humor (typified by their second single, "I Left My Wallet in El Segundo") and underlying cultural nationalism.

Says Q-Tip: "We want to steer clear of trends. Even the pro-Black thing has become just a trend now. A lot of it is phony. With us, it's from the heart. We don't want to gear ourselves to anyone who isn't willing to think for themselves. We're not about force-feeding our peers anything, or settling for something that isn't one hundred percent us."

88

Manhattan, March 1990.

native tongues posse

The Native Tongues Posse is the formal name for an informal group of artists—De La Soul, the Jungle Brothers, Queen Latifah, A Tribe Called Quest, Sister Monie Love—who share an Afrocentric orientation. Along with their affection for African clothing and accessories, they all glow with a characteristic playfulness, funkiness, and spirituality. Whether or not it's fitting to think of them as the hippies of rap, there's no question that the Native Tongues Posse has brought a refreshingly upbeat and cool new vibe to the music.

From the Jungle Brothers' "Doin' Our Own Dang," with De La Soul, Monie Love, and Q-Tip from A Tribe Called Quest

My fam-i-ly sets all the trends
From Soul to Soul on to Loose Ends
A&R men sign groups like them
('Cause that's where the money's at,
    honey!)
Yeah . . .
The industry's filled with copy cats
R&B mixed wit' sloppy raps
Tribes like us always open doors
But what for? So you can get yours?
You ain't into it—all you want is profit
So I ax you please to stop it
Leave me alone. Get off my bone
'Cause I'm doin' my *own* thang.

In comes the mood of jungle and daisys
Play the thang and let the vibes raise me
All hold hands and let's walk about
Form a circle and talk about
Don't follow the path that we're steppin'
Truth to the Soul's what I'm crammin'
Reasons for this is the Family's strong
And like Bob Marley said:
"We're jam-
    min' . . . jammin' . . . jammin' . . ."
Seein's believin'—so see and believe
And let the groove of the new proceed
A whole bunch of love, peace signs and
    fun
So let's do what's got to be done . . .

90

Top: **Queen Latifah.**   Bottom: **Monie Love.**

queen latifah and monie love

From "Ladies First"

QUEEN LATIFAH

The ladies will kick it, the rhyme it is
  wicked
Those who don't know how to be pros get
  evicted
A woman can bear you, break you, take
  you
Now it's time to rhyme. Can you relate to
A sister dope enough to make you holler
  and scream?

MONIE LOVE

Ay, yo! Let me take it from here, Queen!
Excuse me, but I think I'm about due
To get into precisely what I am about to
  do
I'm conversating to the folks who have no
  whatsoever clue
So listen very carefully as I break it down
  for you
Merrily, merrily, merrily, merrily, hyper,
  happy, overjoyed
Pleased with all the beats and rhymes my
  sister has employed
Slick and smooth, throwing down, the
  sound totally a yes
Let me state the position: Ladies first,
  yes?

BOTH
Yes!

Queen Latifah and Monie Love are two of the brightest, strongest, and most dignified young women in rap. Latifah, born Dana Owens in East Orange, New Jersey, was the first female rapper to emerge with an Afrocentric orientation. She started out as the human beat box in a crew of female rappers known as Ladies Fresh. In the fall of 1988, when she was only eighteen years old, she released her first record, "Wrath of My Madness," backed with "Princess of the Posse." Her first album, *All Hail the Queen,* came out in the fall of 1989. In addition to her affiliation with the Native Tongues Posse, the Queen is down with the artistic collaborators who call themselves the Flavor Unit: Lakim Sha-bazz, Chill Rob G, Apache, and DJ Mark, the 45 King (her producer, and an artist in his own right).

On the subject of the sexism of too many male rappers, she's said: "I guess it's there, but I don't see it like everyone else does. When they talk that way, they're not talking about the decent ones, they're talking about the tramps. The rappers don't treat their mothers or their sisters like that. None of them would come up to me and say, 'Latifah, b-i-t-c-h.' I have the utmost respect for them and they for me."

On the subject of American foreign policy, she's said: "I think [America] helps others before it helps itself. We give billions to other countries when our act is not together. We still have homelessness, starvation, drugs, racism, teen-age pregnancy. Can't clean other people's houses before your own, and ours is filthy right now."

Monie Love (born Simone Johnson) is a young British rapper who moved to New York in 1989. She hooked up with the Native Tongues Posse after meeting the Jungle Brothers at a gig in London in September 1988. Almost overnight she was road-managing the JBs on their tour through Europe, and hosting the show. "We just hit it off," she's explained. "It clicked. We were compatible." Monie was featured on the Jungle Brothers' "Doin' Our Own Dang" and De La Soul's "Buddy" prior to the release of her debut album, *Down to Earth* (produced by the Jungle Brothers' Afrika Baby Bambaataa), in the summer of 1990.

92

Clockwise from top left: **Dr. Dre, MC Ren, DJ Yella, and Eazy E. Torrance, California, May 1990.**

nwa

From "[Fuck] tha Police"

Fuck the police, comin' straight from the
    underground
A young nigger got it bad because I'm
    brown
And not the other color. Some police
    think
They have the authority to kill a minority
Fuck that shit 'cause I ain't the one
For a punk motherfucker with a badge and
    a gun
. . . Ice Cube will swarm
On any motherfucker in a blue uniform
Just 'cause I'm from the CPT
Punk police are afraid of me, huh!
A young nigger on the warpath
And when I finish, it's gonna be a blood-
    bath
Of cops dying in L.A.
Yo, Dre, I got something to say:

NWA was the first act from the West Coast ever to earn rap's uncontested heavyweight crown. In February 1989, with the release of "Straight Outta Compton," this five-man crew of Niggers With Attitude from the ghetto just outside Los Angeles brought an abrupt end to ten solid years of East Coast rap dominance. There was simply nothing being cut anywhere else by anyone else to compare with the ice-cold documentary realism of songs like "——— tha Police" or "Gangsta Gangsta."

Everyone who mattered paid their immediate respects: over a million kids quickly bought copies of the album . . . and the FBI launched an unprecedented campaign of harassment. Informed about the lyrics of "——— tha Police" by Bob DeMoss, the "youth culture specialist" of a right-wing religious group called Focus on the Family, the FBI wrote a letter to Priority Records dated August 1, 1989, that complained that the song "encourages violence against and disrespect for the law-enforcement officer." An informal police network then faxed messages to police stations in every city in which the group toured, urging local officers to help cancel concerts by NWA. At tour's end, when the group finally performed the song in concert in Detroit, the police charged the stage. "We just wanted to show the kids that you can't say 'fuck the police' in Detroit," explained one officer.

NWA records for their own label, Ruthless Records, financed by group member Eazy E (once admiringly described as "the Gordon Gekko of Compton" by one of his business colleagues). The other members of the original crew were Dre, Ren, DJ Yella and Ice Cube. Ice Cube left the group early in 1990 in a dispute over money.

Said Ice Cube about "——— tha Police": "There is a lot of resentment of police because, if you are black, you get picked on a lot. They see you in a car with a beeper and they assume you are a dope dealer. The song is a way to get out aggression. We're not really urging anyone to go out and attack police."

Fuck the police!
Fuck the police!
Fuck the police!
Fuck the police!

. . . I'm sayin', "Fuck you, punk!"
Readin' my rights and shit—it's all junk
Pullin' out a silly club so you stand
With a fake-ass badge and a gun in your
  hand
But take off the gun so you can see
  what's up
And we'll go at it, punk, and I'ma fuck
  you up
Make you think I'ma kick your ass
But drop your gat and Ren's gonna blast
I'm sneaky as fuck when it comes to crime
But I'ma smoke 'em now and not next time
Smoke any muthafucka that sweats me
Or any asshole that threatens me
I'm a sniper with a hell of a scope

Takin' out a cop or two that can't cope
  with me
The motherfuckin' villain that's mad
With potential to get bad as fuck
. . . Takin' out a police would make my
  day
But a nigger like Ren don't give a fuck to
  say:

Fuck the police!
Fuck the police!
Fuck the police!
Fuck the police!

. . . The E with the criminal behavior
Yeah, I'm a gangster, but I still got flavor
Without a gun and a badge, what do you
  got?
A sucker in a uniform waiting to get shot
By me or another nigger
And with a gat it don't matter if he's

smaller or bigger
(Size don't mean shit. He's from the old
  school, fool)
And as you all know, E's here to rule
Whenever I'm rollin', keep lookin' in the
  mirror
And ears on cue, Yo!, so you can hear a
Dumb motherfucker with a gun
And if I'm rollin' of the eight, he'll be the
  one
That I take out and then get away
While I'm driving off laughin' this is what
  I'll say:

Fuck the police!
Fuck the police!
Fuck the police!
Fuck the police!

Torrance, California, May 1990.

Inglewood, California, May 1990.

ice cube

From "The Nigga Ya Love to Hate"

"Soul Train" done lost they soul
Just call it train 'cause the bitches look
  like ho's
I seen a lot of others, damn
It almost looked like a Bandstand
You ask me did I like Arsenio
About as much as the Bicentennial
I don't give a fuck about dissin' these
  fools
'Cause they all scared of the Ice Cube
And what I say, what I portray and all that
And ain't even seen the gat
I don't wanna see no dancin'
I'm sick of that shit, listen to the hit
'Cause, yo, if I look and see another
  brother on a video tryin'a outdance
  each other
I'ma tell T-Bone to pass the bottle
And don't give me that shit about role
  models
It ain't wise to chastise and preach
Just open the eyes of each
'Cause laws are meant to be broken up
What niggas need to do is start loc'in' up
And build, mold, fold themselves in the
  shape
Of the nigga ya love to hate!

CHORUS *Fuck you, Ice Cube!*
Yeaaah! Ha-ha! It's the nigga ya love to
  hate!
Fuck you, Ice Cube!
It's the nigga ya love to hate!
VOICE: Yo, you ain't doin' nothin' positive
  for the brothers! What you gotta say for
  yourself?
CUBE: You don't like how I'm livin'? Well,
  fuck you!

Ice Cube, born Oshea Jackson, first made a name for himself in 1988 as the chief lyricist for NWA. A year and a half later he decided he wasn't being fairly compensated for his labors and left the group to go solo. He teamed up with Public Enemy's "Bomb Squad" production team (which includes Chuck D and Hank Shocklee) and issued his debut album, *Amerikkka's Most Wanted*, late in the spring of 1990.

He's said: "This is not just dance music. It's about knowing yourself and knowing who is against you and who is trying to bring you down. I want people to listen to the words. People sometimes act as if we are making up the stuff we talk about on the records, that we are trying to be controversial and shocking. It *is* controversial and shocking, but it's also *real.* We're speaking in the language of the neighborhood. The homeboys know exactly what we're saying ... and it shows them they're not alone.

"Most whites don't know what goes on in this world. They don't even see these streets. The record will be as close as most people get to us.

"People say I'm real negative, but I figure if I teach someone something that they didn't know, that's the most positive thing I can do."

With his mother. Inglewood, California, May 1990.

97

98

Los Angeles, May 1990.

tone loc

From "Funky Cold Medina"

Cold coolin' at the bar and I'm lookin' for
    some action
But like Mick Jagger said, I can't get no
    satisfaction
The girls are all around, but none of them
    want to get with me
My threads are fresh and I'm lookin' def,
    yo, what's up with the L-o-c?
The girls was all jockin' at the other end
    of the bar
Havin' drinks with some no-name chump
    when they know that I'm the star
So I got up and strolled over to the other
    side of the cantina
I asked the guy, "Why are you so fly?" He
    said, "Funky cold medina!"

This brother told me a secret on how to
    get more chicks
Put a little medina in your glass and the
    girls will come real quick
It's better than any alcohol or aphrodisiac
A couple of sips of this love potion and
    she'll be on your lap
So I gave some to my dog when he began
    to beg
Then he licked his bowl and looked at me
    and did the wild thing on my leg
He used to scratch and bite me. Before he
    was much much meaner
Now all the poodles run to my house for
    the funky cold medina.

Tone Loc, one of the most popular and likable figures in the history of Eighties rock, almost never got his shot. "Wild Thing," his first huge smash, was inspired by Fab 5 Freddy fly b-boy come-on to Lola Darling in Spike Lee's *She's Gotta Have It*—"Yo, baby, come up to my house. Let's do the wild thing. Let's get loose!" The record's producers, Delicious Vinyl's Matt Dike and Mike Ross (aka the Dust Brothers), originally wanted to cut it with Fred. When logistical problems prevented him from doing it, they turned to another new artist on the label, Tone Loc.

Born Tony Smith, "Tone Loc" is the shortened form of Tony Loco, the admiring nickname with which the former L.A. gangster had been tagged by his youthful associates. But new nickname, new career, what's the diff? Loc has more than enough personality to spare. His gravelly voice, his laid-back cool, his friendliness, his sense of humor . . . these qualities came through on record and video. And before he knew it, "Wild Thing" was the second-largest-selling single of all time (after "We Are the World"), while his debut album was on its way to becoming the second by a rap act (after the Beasties' "Licensed to Ill") to go to the top of *Billboard*'s Top Pop Albums chart. All of which makes Tone, the Dust Brothers, and Young MC (who wrote Loc's lyrics) seem about as loco as a fox.

In his backyard. Los Angeles, May 1990.

99

young mc

From "Bust a Move"

This here's a jam for all the fellas
Try to do what those ladies tell us
Got shot down 'cause you're overzealous
Play hard-to-get and females get jealous
Okay, smarty, go to a party
Girls are scantily-clad and showing body
A chick walks by, you wish you could sex
   her
But you're standin' on the wall like you
   were Poindexter
Next day's function, high-class luncheon
Food is served and you're stone-cold
   munchin'
Music comes in, people start to dance
But you ate so much you nearly split your
   pants
A girl starts walkin', guys start gawkin'
Sits down next to you and starts talkin'
Says she wants to dance 'cause she like
   the groove
So, come on, Fatso, and just bust a move!

Young MC, on paper, is not the likeliest of hip-hop heroes. He is distinctly clean-cut and bookish-looking, and you'd sooner guess that he was, say, an economics major at UCLA than a rapper. In fact, the English-born, Hollis, Queens–raised Marvin Young *was* an economics major at UCLA. But he was also a behind-the-scenes co-conspirator of the Dust Brothers, and the writer of both "Wild Thing" and "Funky Cold Medina" for Tone Loc.

Out on his own for the first time, he cut "Bust a Move," a great dance track accompanied by a sexy video and—voila!—he was shortly riding one of 1989's biggest singles. Six months down the road the Grammy's named it Best Rap Record of the Year and a few months after that nice guy Young MC was hawking Pepsi on television. If he keeps on at this rate, we may yet see a rapper in the White House.

Left: **Manhattan, March 1990.**

3rd bass

From "Product of the Environment"

MC SERCH

On the streets of Far Rockaway, Queens
Sea Girt Boulevard, Beach Seventeen
Red Fern Houses, where no emcee would
    ever go
Is where I did my very first show
Had the crowd, had the rhymes goin', I
    never 'fessed
My reward was almost a bullet in my chest
And on that stage is where I first learned:
Stick out my chest, or be a kid and get
    burned
You're so foolish, but I think you knew
    this:
That on the microphone, punk, I can do
    this
And doin' this is what life meant
'Cause I'm a product of the environment

PRIME MINISTER PETE NICE

You hear it in the strength of my voice
    and in my rhythm
Now ya know how I was livin'
It happened to me like it happened to
    Serch
Prime Minister Pete Nice'll kick the verse
In Bed-Stuy with my boy, Kipwe-Hype
Decatur and Kingston, Wednesday night
To the Empire, show slammin'
Opened for Dana, crew flammin'
Mouth opened wide, all listening

3rd Bass—like more and more hip young white kids these days—argue that race may be as much a matter of cultural identification as it is of skin color. Growing up in New York City during the Eighties, MC Serch (Michael Berrin) and Peter Nice (Pete Nash) contend that nothing could have been more natural than the expression of their musical and lyrical talents in the form of rap. They'd each made records separately when producer Sam Sever suggested they team up in 1988.

Says Pete: "I went to Columbia University and took a lot of classes in modern poetry. To me, rap is modern poetry. There's a lot going on that you might not even notice at first. We say a lot in our records, but you'll have to dig into it in order to find the multiple meanings."

Says Serch: "Some stuff is real clear and we get the point across real swift. We want to break a lot of the stereotypes that have been set upon the black community, and I think the way we do it is kind of intelligent. We're not punching you in the face, telling you that we're black—we're *not* black, we're white— but our love and respect for the black community runs deep. Public Enemy's latest album is called *Fear of a Black Planet,* and I just want to say that we have no fear of a black planet. Bring it on."

Dumb-dope with a forty in my system
Unprotected, but respected for my own
    self
'Cause of talent, no shade or nothing else
A time of tension, racially fenced-in
I came off (and all the brothers blessed
    him)
I left more than a mark, I left a dent
'Cause I'm a product of the environment

Left. Left to right: **DJ Richie Rich, Pete Nice, and Serch. At "Rapmania," 1990.**

Ultramagnetic MC's. Manhattan, 1989.

informed sources

The following monthly publications are devoted exclusively to rap and/or to the fight against music censorship. We recommend them to the attention of all of our readers.

Black Beat
Sterling's Magazine
35 Wilbur St.
Lynbrook, NY 11563
$20/year

Hip-Hop Connection
Alexander House
Forehill
Ely, Cambridgeshire
England CB74AF
$60/year

Rapmasters
63 Grand Ave.
River Edge, NJ 07661
$24/year

Right On!
Sterling's Magazine
35 Wilbur St.
Lynbrook, NY 11563
$20/year

Rock 'n' Roll Confidential
Box 341305
Los Angeles, CA 90034
$24/year ($33/year, foreign)

The Source
594 Broadway
New York, NY 10012-3233
$19.95/year

Street Sound
427 Yonge Street
Toronto, Ontario M5B1T1
$30/year in US and Canada, $55/year foreign

Yo!
P.O. Box 88427
Los Angeles, CA 90009
$20/year

Top row, left to right: **Sparky D, Sweet T, Yvette Money, and Ms. Melodie.** *Middle row, left to right:* **Millie Jackson, Peaches, and [Sparky D dancer number one].** *Bottom row, left to right:* **[Sparky D dancer number two], Roxanne Shante, MC Lyte, and Synquis.** At *Paper* magazine's "Rap Round-table," Manhattan, May 1988.

Flavor Flav. Manhattan, 1987.